PRAYER
A Gift of Life

PETER HOCKEN

PAULIST PRESS
New York / Paramus, N.J. / Toronto

First published in Great Britain in 1974 by
Darton, Longman & Todd Ltd.,
85 Gloucester Road, London, SW7 4SU

©Peter Hocken, 1974

ISBN 0-8091-0199-8

Published in the United States of America by Paulist Press
Editorial Office: 1865 Broadway, N.Y., N.Y. 10023
Business Office: 400 Sette Drive, Paramus, N.J. 07652

Printed and bound in the
United States of America

CONTENTS

Prayer, a Gift of Life	9
Praying in Christ	15
Responding to God's Word	27
Sharing in Prayer	38
Praying with Faith	53
Growth in the Spirit	69
Praise and Thanksgiving	78
Silence and Sound	91
The Discernment of Spirits	101
God, the Giver of Tasks	113
God, the Breaker of Idols	122

PREFACE

It is no secret that this book on prayer reflects the influence, and I hope the impact, of the Pentecostal movement. Many other Christians, touched by this same impulse of the Holy Spirit, have written books and pamphlets about Pentecostal prayer, the charismatic renewal, the gifts of the Spirit, etc. It is an unfortunate though largely unintended consequence of that approach that the impression is given that the Holy Spirit is a *plus* factor; you have ordinary Christian prayer, and then you have 'prayer in the Spirit' or charismatic prayer.

It is my firm conviction that every new coming of God's Spirit enlivens and deepens every previous coming of the Spirit. All spiritual progress is deeper entry into the one mystery, the person of Jesus Christ. The Spirit brings alive all we have already been given; the Spirit makes fresh what has become stale, puts new flesh on old bones, and causes new life to pulse through the old body.

I have therefore deliberately not written a book about Pentecostal prayer or praying in groups, but I have tried to present a total Christian view of prayer, so that what is said covers all forms of praying, liturgical and non-liturgical, communal and individual, verbal and non-verbal. The chapter-headings do not I think reflect anything particularly Pentecostal; but it is unlikely that they would have been so entitled had I not made contact with Pentecostal Christians. My presentation is of course based on a particular theological understanding of the work of the Holy Spirit in the Church, but this has not been made explicit as the book is wholly aimed at promoting prayer and is only indirectly concerned with promoting theological understanding.

Whilst I have written primarily for Roman Catholic readers, the passages which presume familiarity with their liturgy, theology and/or devotional practice are, I hope, neither so frequent nor so essential for understanding the points being made as to deter readers from other Christian traditions.

Prayer, A Gift of Life

Prayer is the gift of God to man. It is the gift of eternal life, the gift by which we live as sons of the Father: 'You have received the spirit of sonship. When we cry "Abba, Father" it is the Spirit himself bearing witness with our spirit that we are children of God' (Rom. 8:15–16). To live as a son is to be one who cries out to his Father. To believe is to pray.

Life depends on relationships. 'This is eternal life, that they know thee the only true God, and Jesus Christ whom thou hast sent.' (John 17:3) Prayer is our reception of this relationship with the Father through Jesus Christ; it is the acknowledgment and deepening of our sonship. So we receive the gift of life which is the Spirit. Friendship and love are our life-blood, and for Christians 'our fellowship is with the Father and with his Son Jesus Christ' (1 John 1:3).

We believe by faith that all life comes from God, and that in every breath we are sustained by his creative power; in the Nicene Creed we profess our faith that the Holy Spirit is the giver of life. The Spirit is that more abundant life that Jesus came to give; he is that breath of life that leads everything that breathes to praise the Lord (cf. Ps. 150:6). Every step towards the Father into Christ is the fruit of the Spirit.

Learning to pray is then learning to receive the gift that God is giving now, learning to live what is being given now, learning to hear and to do the Word of God that is being spoken now. 'Man shall not live by bread alone, but by every word that proceeds from the mouth of God.' (Matt. 4:4). This is life, and this is faith: to turn consciously to receive the living Word that proceeds from the mouth of the Father. 'My mother and my brothers' says Jesus 'are those who hear the Word of God and do it.' (Luke 8:21)

Real praying is real living, and the gateway to life. True prayer does not lead us away from life; rather it puts us in living touch with the Creator and source of all life. The sort of praying that is an escape from living (and contemplative prayer is a fuller form of living not an escape) is a caricature of prayer, for it has lost touch with the living God.

Prayer and life go together, as trust and love go together. All require faith, a going out from ourselves, an abandonment of our self-sufficiency, a change in our centre of gravity: and in God as manifest in Jesus Christ we have found the true Centre, the source of all, the One in whom alone absolute trust is to be placed.

In Jesus Christ, we find all these characteristics at their most intense—the living by every word that proceeds from the mouth of the Father, absolute trust in the Father, and the most complete self-giving in love. Jesus brings life, because he is most fully alive: and so St. John tells us that he is the way, the truth and the life. (cf. 14:6)

Growing in prayer is then growing in faith and trust; it is learning to live. Immediately we assimilate learning to pray to learning to do things, to learning a technique, then we have lost the way; we are on the road of self-deception, of erecting idols in place of the living God. Throughout this book, what is presented is the structure of life itself, the structure of human living, as coming from and being drawn into the structure of God's living. So we learn to receive the life that God is giving, and we receive it in thanksgiving. We learn to love, to trust, to have confidence, to accept the other, to listen, to respond; in prayer we receive the capacity and power so to live, being caught up into the life of God, their source and exemplar.

Why is it that we don't readily associate praying with

living, that for many people praying is more readily linked with death than with life?

Here we can point both to the fact of sin, and to defective presentations of prayer. The existence of sin will always mean that what looks like death is really life, and what looks like life is really death; the attraction of sin is that it purports to bring life, it presents a mirage of the good life, and like every mirage it evaporates into nothing. The apparent success of the wicked is a theme found throughout the Scriptures; the life of sin will always appear as real life, and the life of the holy as death and folly.

But this is the worldly view of things, which the coming of God's Spirit shows up as illusion; this distorted view of reality should not prevail in the life of any Christian. That it does so is partly attributable to inadequate presentations of prayer, and it is in the hope of helping to remedy this situation that this book has been written.

A major defect has been the emphasis on prayer as a duty, more frequently the duty owed by a creature to the Creator than that of Christians to their Father. Appeals to duty always suggest an element of despair, as though all other forms of persuasion hold little hope of success. And so for many children saying their prayers becomes one of those unpleasant duties, like writing thank-you letters, cleaning teeth, doing homework, taking medicine, which adults present as necessary chores leading to untold benefits in an unspecified future. So the impression is given that prayer is a bore, an activity you couldn't imagine wanting to do, that you don't expect to do any good, or to make any difference to your real life.

With the duty and drudgery impression goes the ready confusion of prayer with saying prayers, and insufficient attention being given to what we are seeking. In helping people to pray, a key question is whether they are seeking God. Difficulties in praying may stem from wrong seeking. Suggesting that prayer will always be sweat and toil overlooks the gift-aspect of prayer, and can encourage too intense an approach. Those who are not put off by the sweat and toil emphasis can end up trying too hard; we can get on our knees resolving 'I'm going to succeed in this or bust'. So we grit our teeth, and work up a grim determination, as though prayer depends on our strength of will, and God could be bent to our moulding.

The close connection between prayer and life, between praying and living, becomes tenuous whenever the Holy Spirit is neglected. For the biblical terms for spirit (the Hebrew *ruah* and the Greek *pneuma*) signify movement of the air, breeze, wind and thus also breath and life. The God of the Old Covenant is he 'who spread forth the earth and what comes from it, who gives breath to the people upon it, and spirit to those who walk in it' (Is. 42:5). So the Spirit of God, the promise and gift of the Father, brings the life of God: 'for the written code kills, but the Spirit gives life' (2 Cor. 3:6). So in the Christian life, the coming of the Spirit brings existence alive; this enlivening, foretold in Ezekiel's vision of the valley of dry bones (37:1-14), is beautifully summarised in the Latin hymn, *Veni, Sancte Spiritus*, from the liturgy of Pentecost:

> *Lava quod est sordidum, riga quod est aridum,*
> *sana quod est saucium;*
> *Flecte quod est rigidum, fove quod est frigidum,*
> *rege quod est devium.*

The crispness and sharp contrast in the Latin are somewhat lost in English translation:

> *Heal our wounds, our strength renew;*
> *on our dryness pour thy dew;*
> *Wash the stains of guilt away:*
> *Bend the stubborn heart and will;*
> *Melt the frozen, warm the chill;*
> *Guide the steps that go astray.*

The approach adopted in this book is, I believe, faithful to the New Testament and to the basic Catholic tradition; it is rooted in the complementarity of the action of God and the action of man: that God gives, and man receives, but with asking and seeking as part of man's receiving.

Every presentation of prayer is based upon a view of God and a view of man. A Christian presentation must be based on the Christian vision of God, as revealed in Jesus Christ by the action of the Holy Spirit. The inadequate presentations of prayer here criticised imply a less than Christian understanding of God. So we can ask ourselves: what image of God is implicit in the way we pray? Is this image of God the person of Jesus Christ? Is the God we worship he who seeks out the lost sheep, the father who runs to greet the prodigal son, the host who invites to his banquet from the highways and the hedgerows?

What impressions of God and of the Lordship of Jesus Christ lie behind the duty-talk and the toil-approach? Of someone who is rather indifferent to our efforts? or someone whose attention is rather hard to catch and whose mind is on other things? It is true that God's sons have to suffer; as the Epistle to the Hebrews says: 'God is treating you as sons; for what son is there whom his father does not discipline?' (12:7). But the discipline of a loving Father always occurs in a context of experienced love; and we are called to believe in a God whose fatherhood excels all that we know of human fatherhood. 'If you then, who are evil, know how to give good gifts to your children, how much more will the heavenly Father give the Holy Spirit to those who ask him!' (Luke 11:13).

Even when we were dead, God has made us alive, St. Paul tells the Ephesians (2:1–5). The Father has restored us to life by sending his only Son. 'And from his fulness have we all received, grace upon grace.' (John 1:16). Loving communion with the Father is at the heart of this fulness, and God longs to lavish this upon us; so he is calling us to pray, prodding us to pray, reaching out to give us prayer if we will receive. Our convictions about prayer follow from our convictions about God; and our convictions about God grow through the conviction of prayer. Oremus, et vivamus. Let us pray, and live.

Praying in Christ

The life that the Father gives is the life of his only Son Jesus Christ; and the life of Jesus is given through the power of the Holy Spirit. Prayer in Christ to the Father by the power of the Spirit is the pattern of all Christian prayer; it is summed up in the concluding doxology of the Canon of the Mass: 'Through him, with him, in him, in the unity of the Holy Spirit, all glory and honour is yours, almighty Father, for ever and ever.'

This pattern is a structure of life manifesting the life of God, rather than a rubric forbidding direct address to the Son or the Spirit. The liturgy of the Church illustrates the pattern, but violates the rubric; for whilst some prayers are addressed directly to Christ and to the Spirit (e.g. *Christe eleison* and *Veni, Sancte Spiritus*), the basic pattern found in the presidential prayers (the Collect, the prayer over the Offerings, and the Post communion, as well as the Eucharistic Prayer itself) is *ad Patrem*. So when we do address the Son or the Spirit, we do so in the awareness that Christ is the way to the Father, and the Spirit is the Spirit of the Father and of the Son.

Understanding the intra-Trinitarian character of Christian prayer is not a matter of getting our addresses right, but concerns the formation of an explicitly Christian consciousness, of our being sons of the Father in his only Son Jesus Christ. We can now consider some of the consequences of this pattern for Christian prayer.

The Prayer of Christ. The intra-Trinitarian pattern means

first that Christian prayer is Jesus Christ praying in us. Jesus draws us into his movement to the Father, and so into his prayer. 'Truly, truly, I say to you, he who believes in me will also do the works that I do' (John 14:12); and at the heart of the works done by Jesus is his prayer to the Father.

Thus to be given the life of Christ is to be given a share in his prayer. Learning to pray is allowing that prayer of Jesus to well up within us. To place ourselves in the presence of God, in the traditional phrase, is to become aware of Christ within us; to become aware of Christ is to face the Father, and to face the Father is to have the awareness of Christ.

Christian prayer is not just aimed outwards and upwards; it is not the sending of a message from here to there. There is no one's attention to be gained, except our own; for we are within the portals, with Jesus Christ within us. In that sense, we pray because we have arrived; we act because the action is already on. For wherever Jesus Christ is present, he is praying: 'he holds his priesthood permanently, because he continues for ever. Consequently he is able for all time to save those who draw near to God through him, since he always lives to make intercession for them' (Heb. 7:24-25). He lives in us, and he prays in us: but how intensely depends on how much we open to him, and join in his life and prayer. Starting to pray is coming alive to what is already going on, namely the prayer of Jesus Christ.

Much teaching on praying the prayer of Christ can be found in the writings of the Abbé Paul Couturier, that great apostle of Christian unity, who died in 1953. Couturier insisted that all Christians could be united in prayer for unity, despite their different notions of what that unity might be, by all praying the prayer of Christ 'that they may all be one' (John 17:21). For Christian unity can only be realised by doing the Father's will, and being made one in the body of Jesus Christ. Here we are taking up the central idea of Couturier, not just as the right way to pray for Christian unity, but as the right way for Christians to pray at any time.

Within the Lordship of Christ. This Jesus within whom we pray is the risen Jesus, whom the Father has made both Lord and Saviour. Christian prayer is made within this Lordship of Jesus Christ, and in his victorious Name.

Through baptism we are members of the body of which Jesus is the head, and living stones of that Temple of which he is the corner-stone. In the resurrection of Jesus, humanity and so human prayer have found acceptance with the Father. Being in him, we are already accepted. This is why when we pray in the name of Jesus, the Father grants our requests: 'Whatever you ask in my name, I will do it, that the Father may be glorified in the Son' (John 14:13).

This 'already achieved' aspect of life in Christ is taught by St. Paul in some startling passages, whose force too easily escapes us. For St. Paul, the Christian is both one who is now established with Christ at the right hand of the Father, and one who is still running the race and fighting the good fight. 'But God, who is rich in mercy, out of the great love with which he loved us, even when we were dead through our trespasses, made us alive together with Christ (by grace you have been saved), and raised us up with him, and made us sit with him in the heavenly places in Christ Jesus' (Eph. 2:4-6). This teaching is also found in Colossians: 'If then you have been raised with Christ, seek the things that are above, where Christ is, seated at the right hand of God . . . For you have died, and your life is hid with Christ in God. When Christ who is our life appears, then you also will appear with him in glory' (3:1, 3-4).

To be baptised and to become a member of the body of Christ, is to be where Christ is. We are marked with his sign, the death and resurrection by which he returned to his Father. The end is contained in the beginning; we have to become what we are. 'In him you also, who have heard the word of truth, the gospel of your salvation, and have believed in him, were sealed with the promised Holy Spirit, which is the guarantee of our inheritance until we acquire possession of it, to the praise of his glory' (Eph. 1:13-14).

Praying in Christ is consciously living this paradox of the already and the not yet. This is the tension of praying in faith, praying with the conviction that we are now with Christ and Christ with us, yet knowing too that we walk by faith and not by sight, that we are still pilgrims on the way, pilgrims who sin and err. Holding this tension means avoiding the two extremes: on the one hand, praying as those who only err, praying on a hit or miss basis, just leaving it to God to grant or not, as though we are not his instruments in the praying; and, on the other hand, praying as though our will is identical with God's will, by-passing the need for discernment but this time through the false certainty of presumption.

This tension between the already and not yet (of our identification with Christ) shows up in the way that the power of the Spirit of God comes and goes. There are times in our prayer, when we sense the surging of the Spirit within, and we feel our prayer can sweep all before us; and yet there are also times when we feel empty, when we are like a becalmed yacht, motionless until the breeze gets up. Such variations we must learn to accept; for the periods of calm, the moments of apparent absence, remind us of God's transcendence, that the coming is his free gift and is not within our control. But the power is there when it is needed, even though we may not feel it; for we must believe that when the Lord gives a task, even the giving of the humblest prayer, he gives the impetus and the strength. So when we have nothing to say, we should not worry; for we will have something to say when it is right to speak. 'When they bring you before the synagogues and the rulers and the authorities, do not be anxious how or what you are to answer or what you are to say; for the Holy Spirit will teach you in that very hour what you ought to say' (Luke

12:11–12). We may surely assume that Jesus' extreme example of persecution was chosen because of the greater temptation to doubt and anxiety then present, not because it is the only occasion on which the Holy Spirit will give us words. The Spirit is with the Christian all the time; and he will lead us always if we let him. So we discover when we need to speak and have the power, and when we do not need to speak, but have to remain silent in the Lord.

Being Conformed to Christ. Progress in prayer is then growth into the prayer of Christ. As we grow in Christ, we see people more with his eyes, we hear more with his ears and love more with his heart; so that we come to share his sorrow for sin and ingratitude, and to share his rejoicing over every sinner who repents. We thus come to share more fully in the range of Jesus' prayer from the agonising prayer of Gethsemane to the transfiguration prayer of Mount Tabor.

In baptism we are marked with the death and resurrection of Jesus Christ; and that is the pattern to which we are being conformed. It includes both a share in the cup of Christ's suffering, and an anticipation of future glorification.

Transfiguration moments are experiences of anticipation, when our Father is showing us momentarily what we are to become, where he is leading us. Our prayer at such times is an instance of the vital truth that in one sense we are already there. These moments are of great importance, and are a complementary personal prefiguring in experience to that expressed in the communal sacramental actions of the Church; such moments strengthen us, give us a vision of God's plan, and provide powerful support in subsequent times of desolation, suffering and abandonment. They should not be treated as 'mere consolations', for this overlooks the prefiguring element; nor should they be written off as emotional feelings of no importance, for that also overlooks the significance of such experiences. But equally they are not to be mistaken for achievement; and much anxiety is caused by making this mistake, and subsequent wondering what has gone wrong when the experience is over.

Indeed these God-given moments of exaltation are often followed quite closely by periods of humiliation and experiences of impotence. It is surely not a coincidence that St. Matthew presents in turn the Lord's blessing on Simon Peter and his confession of faith, the incident in which Jesus says to Peter 'Get behind me, Satan', the teaching on the need to take up the cross and follow Christ, the account of the Transfiguration, and the disciples' inability to cast out a demon because of their little faith. After the exaltation and exhilaration of the mountain-top, we need to be reminded that 'we have this treasure in earthen vessels to show that the transcendent power belongs to God and not to us' (2 Cor. 4:7). So St. Paul says of his own experiences 'to keep me from being too elated by the abundance of revelations, a thorn was given me in the flesh, a messenger of Satan, to harass me, to keep me from being too elated' (2 Cor. 12:7). These attacks, the devil's kick-back, are not a denial but a confirmation of what God has done and that what he has done is beyond our natural comprehension and capacities.

We must live permanently in the victory of Jesus Christ, confident that he has won the victory, that he is Lord now and always. But the victory will be more tangible at some times than at others; and when we have been overwhelmed at some time by the power and majesty of God we have to learn that we cannot 'turn it on', and that we cannot ourselves create the victory mood. Here too we have to follow the way of Jesus; to seek only his Father's Kingdom, and to subordinate all else to that. We see this clearly in the temptations of Jesus, in which he refuses to call upon the power of God for anything but the fulfilment of the Father's will and of his own vocation. We find it again in the Garden of Gethsemane, when Jesus says 'Do you think that I cannot appeal to my Father, and he will at once send me more than twelve legions of angels?' (Matt. 26:53). In the desolation, we must be confident of triumph, that the victory has been won, that the strength and the power will return; but we must not pretend, or attempt to create our own victory independently of what the Lord is giving.

The phases in this growth are considered in the chapter on 'Growth in the Spirit'. Here the point being made is that such growth conforms us to the pattern of Jesus Christ: that there is a fundamental similarity in pattern, the same in all things save sin.

Prophetic Prayer. As we learn to speak the words of Jesus to his Father, so will we begin to speak his words to our fellow men. There is convergence between prophetic prayer and the prophetic word. St. John gives us the words of Jesus 'for I have given them the words which thou gavest me' (17:8), and this includes words to God in prayer as well as words to men in prophecy. The close link between the two is shown by the virtual inter-changeability for the prophet between the intercessory form ('May the Lord forgive you your sins') and the authoritative declaration ('Your sins are forgiven'). Thus when Elisha tells Naaman 'Go, wash and be clean' this is declaring in the name of God, which is stronger in form than 'Go, wash, and may the Lord make you clean'. When we exchange the kiss of peace at Mass, is our formula 'Peace be with you' a prayer or a declaration? It is a greeting, but it is also a prayer. So we find in the ministry of Jesus many declaratory and imperative formulae: 'Rise up', 'Take up your bed and walk', 'Be open'. The pattern is clear in the account of the raising of Lazarus (John 11:38–43).

This closeness of prophetic prayer and prophetic word is a very practical question for our prayer, particularly for priests. For does not growth in our faith lead us beyond the rather uncommitted 'Father, if it be your will, grant this to your servant' to the omission of conditional clauses and the greater firmness of 'Be this, in the name of the Lord'? It is here that the tension in Christian prayer between prayer as expressing God's will, and prayer as expressing man's desire, is fully experienced.

An obvious area of application is that of exorcism, in which evil spirits are commanded to depart in the name of Jesus Christ. The liturgy of the Church contains many declaratory formulae of lesser drama than the rite of exorcism, but which nonetheless express the same firmness of command in faith, e.g. the formulae of baptism and of absolution, in which there is utter confidence in the efficacy of the Word of God, and that the prayer prayed is from the Lord.

These comments are not a recommendation to experiment with declaratory forms in prayer, but they should remind us that progress in prayer will lead us to experience this tension between the intercessory and the imperative, between the 'may' and the 'be', and so we have to be open to the Lord prompting us in deeper faith to simply declare and command in his Name.

This will show us that such formulae are not restricted to the official prayers of Church ritual, but should be a regular part of Christian prophetic ministry; then we will come to realise the depth of faith expressed in the formulae of the sacraments, and get beyond a 'right formulae work' approach that is lacking as an expression of living faith.

Within the Body of Christ. Prayer being in Christ means that it is linked with the prayer of others, for 'the body does not consist of one member but of many' (1 Cor. 12:14). Growth is not just my personal growth as an isolated unit, but is part of the upbuilding of the body 'until we all attain to the unity of the faith and of the knowledge of the Son of God, to mature manhood, to the measure of the stature of the fullness of Christ' (Eph. 4:13). The way in which all our prayer is related to the prayer of our fellow believers, and the way in which private prayer is complementary to prayer with others are considered in the chapter on 'Sharing in Prayer'.

The richness of the Trinitarian pattern. The trinitarian pattern of God's life and of our prayer brings together in a higher synthesis all the positive strands in different religious traditions. Thus Christian worship integrates elements both from the more spiritual religions (e.g. Zen Buddhism) and from the more earthy cults (e.g. the cults of tribes surrounding the Israelites); the tension between the two persisting in Christian history is illustrated in what we may call the Quaker and the Pentecostal poles.

The more spiritual emphasis favours inwardness, silence, contemplation, privacy; it tends to demote words, prophecy, intercession, community and mission. It will promote training in total repose, postures for complete relaxation and emptying of the mind; such traditions focus attention on what is already within man, at the inner point of his being. The ideal then becomes exclusion of the world around and total inner recollection; different traditions here posit different contents to this state, some more negative, emphasising the emptying out, others more positive emphasising the filling that follows. But if this is the whole truth about prayer, it is hard to see how ritual and liturgy have any proper place, how any breaking of silence is other than a concession to the weakness of human nature.

The more earthy religions tend in the opposite direction; they will favour words, intercession, ritual and community, giving a lesser place, if any, to silence and contemplative forms of prayer. They often focus on God as outside, localised in some visible symbol, totem or idol, before whom man bows down and adores. Such traditions will have a strong community sense, with the cult-object being venerated by a tribe or a people; the emphasis will then be on legal and ritual rather than moral requirements for proper worship.

A similar classification can be made distinguishing between traditions emphasising the immanence of God, and those stressing his transcendence; and the same point can be made by considering traditions regarding prayer and worship as being basically 'in God' and those seeing it as 'to God'.

In Jesus Christ all have been made one. The Incarnation unites the divine and the human, the spiritual and the earthy. Immanence and transcendence are fused in Jesus Christ.

So the natural religion found in the prayer 'to' traditions finds its true visible symbol of God in the incarnate Son, who reveals the face of the Father; and it brings the whole community ritual aspect of religion to its purification and consummation. Likewise the real spiritual values in the prayer 'in' traditions find their true place in Christian contemplation of the Father revealed in Jesus Christ; here emptying of the mind and yogic practices find their proper place in the Trinitarian structure of life and prayer. The argument of some secularising theologians that prayer can only be in God, and not to God, manifests a loss of the incarnate and trinitarian structure; Christian prayer is both in and to God, more precisely being in Christ to the Father.

This bringing together in Christ of the earthy and the spiritual means that there is an inter-action between them reflecting the mission of the Son from and to the Father. For the Christian, praise is in Christ, has its own inwardness, and its communal expression, and is to the Father; and it needs prolongation and further internalising in private prayer and silence. But within this silence, words may be formed, as the Logos comes forth from the Father.

This inter-action means that it is wrong to give an absolute priority to the wordless and silent, as though the material and visible is merely a phase we pass through in order to transcend. Jesus does not leave his humanity behind, but in it he is glorified. Here it is significant that the revealed religion of God starts from the earthy, from the typical forms of tribal cult, and purifies, deidolises, from that base. But the base is never left behind; for that is rooted in the materiality of man, in the dust from which he is made.

The complete self-offering of Jesus Christ to his Father is also his self-giving to all men; and therefore the Christian life of contemplating the Father includes the task of intercession. Our personal going to the Father neither leaves behind nor forgets our brother men.

It is not then surprising that those who get the trinitarian pattern wrong have imbalances in their prayer. It is noticeable, for example, that those who pray regularly to Jesus with little advertence to the Father tend to use words constantly and to have little appreciation of silence. Whereas those who pray to God without distinction of person tend to over-privilege silent contemplative prayer, to devalue liturgy and to treat intercessory prayer as intrinsically less perfect.

The trinitarian pattern is then important in determining the areas of legitimate choice in Christian prayer. For all that has been said of the more earthy and the more spiritual emphases forms part of incarnate Christian prayer; and we cannot legitimately choose one to the exclusion of the other. This is important, since we normally have a temperamental bias one way or the other: to be a private contemplative or a liturgical communitarian. We are all called to be both, for there alone is Christian fullness.

There is an ambiguity in the advice sometimes given to 'do what you find helpful'. This formula is, I suggest, a confused form of the sound advice, given by Dom John Chapman, to 'pray as you can, not as you can't'. For 'do what you find helpful' may be an invitation to rationalise our biases, to ignore and dismiss the things we fear; but it is these gaps in our spirituality and our personality that need filling if we are to be whole. Thus no Christian can rightfully say 'I am not a liturgical type, I prefer to stay on my own, it suits my nature' or 'I am a community person myself, a bit of an extrovert, and praying on my own gets me down; the liturgy is enough for me.'

We need to distinguish what is part of being truly human,

from what goes with being a particular type of person with a particular vocation and place in the Church. The former are for all; and choice can only rightly be made in regard to the latter, in what is particular to some but not to all.

As an illustration, we can contrast the gifts of the Spirit and the fruit of the Spirit in the teaching of St. Paul. The gifts, of which examples are given in 1 Corinthians 12:8–11 and Romans 12:6–8, are made to some for the sake of all: as St. Paul says: 'To each is given the manifestation of the Spirit for the common good' (1 Cor. 12:7). And the same is true of the vocations noted in 1 Cor. 12:28 and Eph. 4:11. It is in this context that St. Paul compares the Christians in the Church to the members of a human body, as fulfilling complementary functions within the one organism (cf. 1 Cor. 12:14–26). These rightly ground different though complementary ways of Christian living, according to particular vocations and functions. By contrast, the fruit of the Spirit, with all the characteristics listed in Gal. 5:22–23, is to be looked for in every Christian, though their respective intensity may vary according to individual temperament. All these are part of being truly Christian and truly human.

Thus we have spheres of rightful choice, and spheres in which we have no choice but to be fully Christian. And everything that belongs to the basic trinitarian structure is part of that essentially Christian: and, in that sphere, choice between different forms is literally heresy.

Responding to God's Word

All Christian prayer is response to God's Word under the impulse of the Holy Spirit. The Bible is basic to Christian prayer, and we deliberately link together the various meanings of 'the Word of God', including both the written word which is the Bible that leads up to and expresses the life of the personal Word, who is Jesus Christ.

Jesus is the way to the Father, the one mediator between God and men. To come to the Father, we must seek to know and love Jesus Christ, and to hear him; and this cannot be done without familiarity with the Scriptures. In this chapter we consider the role of the Word of God, particularly the Bible, in the rise and growth of Christian prayer.

Evangelisation and Prayer. Christian prayer is our response to hearing the Word of God addressed to us. The Gospel is announced to us and we hear the good news of salvation; Christian prayer begins with the response of acceptance, when we welcome the Lord into our hearts.

Lack of adequate evangelisation lies behind much difficulty in praying; and whereas in past ages, more could be presumed in the way of general evangelisation, this is no longer possible. It is a mistake to assume that any Catholic who has made his first confession and communion therefore knows how to pray, even though he may know some prayers. Nor do we help the unevangelised by talking to them about prayer; for prayer is not produced by telling people what to do. We can in this way help people to be silent, we can teach them to relax and to achieve a state of mental repose, but we cannot so teach prayer. For prayer is produced by speaking about God, by telling of his mighty deeds, centred on the life of Jesus Christ; it results from speaking the Word, from hearing the Word, from reading the Scriptures, from hearing a prophetic word, from hearing the word of prayer in others. Praying is caught, not taught, as has often been said of religion in general.

There is no short cut in learning to pray that by-passes evangelisation and repentance. Thus by itself getting young people together to pray in a group will not help, unless they can already pray; for you can only share prayer when you can pray. Gathering people into groups when they haven't yet heard the Word of God may result only in their sharing their inability to pray, with an empty silence following. Inviting people to communal prayer with Christians who have received the Word is of course a different matter; for this is to introduce them to a potentially evangelising situation. In this setting one can catch a feel for God from those who are praying.

So we need more talk about God, and less about prayer. For talking about prayer can all too easily treat God as an object within the projected exercise, and it is inherently less costly than talking about God. It can be one way in which we impersonalise the most personal, and begin to talk in terms of methods and techniques, as though learning to pray were like learning to swim or learning to drive.

Repentance and Prayer. The preaching of the Word involves a call to repentance and change of heart. Peter's sermon at Pentecost results in the hearers being 'cut to the heart' (Acts 2:37), and the apostle says to them: 'Repent, and be baptised every one of you in the name of Jesus Christ for the forgiveness of your sins; and you shall receive the gift of the Holy Spirit' (Acts 2:38).

One of the unfortunate results of telling young people at the outset that all praying will be hard work is that it confuses the difficulty of initial repentance with the problems of enduring perseverance which come much later. Speaking of difficulty at the outset can boost reluctance to face the demands of God for conversion of heart; we can then encourage people to keep it up (when 'it' consists of maintaining known prayers and procedures) when their hearts have not really been touched. We then wrongly attribute dryness to the nature of prayer rather than to lack of conversion.

This repentance that is part of Christian faith has a total character; it is dying to sin and rising to new life. This total aspect is expressed by St. Paul in speaking of baptism as burial with Christ into death, so as to be united with him in his resurrection (cf. Rom. 6:3-11). Repentance is much more than just being sorry for having done this and having said that, coupled with good resolutions on these points.

We can only pray to the extent that we have died to sin, and become a new creation: to the extent that we die to self and let God in. The Bible constantly confronts us with the absoluteness of God's love and with his constancy: thus confronted by the Word of God, we are always convicted of sin. When the Spirit comes, he convinces the world of sin (cf. John 16:8). Measuring ourselves against human lists of duties and faults, we can sometimes acquit ourselves; confronted by the Word of God, we are always convicted, and have to acknowledge our sin.

Priests sometimes hear Catholic people saying that they have nothing to confess, because they have not really done anything wrong. Such remarks show an absence of exposure to God's Word, and a measuring of self by human standards, however elevated, rather than by the Word of God. And they can hardly be reassuring signs as to the focus of their prayer.

True repentance is centred on God; it results from deeper turning to God, rather than from closer inspection of ourselves. It should become a constant dimension of our prayer, one with our gratitude and our praise to God, our forgiving Father. Repentance is not just something we do after sin; it flows from every hearing of the Word, and from being with the Lord. To come closer to him is always to know more acutely our own sin and weakness; the prayer of contrition is not something occasional, but a continual dimension of our prayer, that comes into greater focus at particular times.

Eschatological Prayer. Only a firm rooting in the Bible will give our prayer its true eschatological balance. Whilst the word 'eschatology' is used of any theory of the *eschata*, the last things, and so of any orientation to the end of time and the last days, the true Christian understanding has a particular balance between the past, the present and the future. The New Testament presents the Incarnation of Jesus Christ as fulfilling the Old Testament prophecies concerning the last days; with Jesus the end-time has begun. Yet the *full* Old Testament expectation of the Kingdom of God still awaits completion with the second Coming, the return of Jesus Christ in glory and triumph. So Christians pray within this phase of history, in the 'time-between' the two comings, the 'already' and the 'not yet' mentioned in the chapter 'Praying in Christ'.

The Bible helps us to get our tenses right in prayer; we learn the balance between 'The Lord has done it', 'The Lord is doing it' and 'The Lord will do it'. For all Christian prayer is made in the light of God's past deeds, with their climax in the resurrection of Jesus Christ and the outpouring of the Holy Spirit on the Church, and in the hope and confident expectation of the final fulfilment when Christ will be all in all. We always pray 'as we wait in joyful hope for the coming of our Saviour Jesus Christ' (from the prayer *Libera nos* in the Roman Missal).

This time-framework, illustrated in the relationship between the two Testaments, Old and New, and in the way in which the New still looks to future completion, provides the basis for balancing the elements of memorial and thanksgiving, on the one hand, and of anticipation and intercession, on the other hand. Only when we are solidly grounded in the

Bible, both Old and New Testaments, can our prayer acquire this distinctively Christian time-context, rightly relating past, present and future and so reflect the truths in both realised eschatology (God's Kingdom being realised here and now) and future eschatology (God's Kingdom coming at the end of the ages). We are introduced to this time-framework in the whole liturgy of the Church, in the tenses of prayer, in the use of the lectionary and in the arrangement of the calendar.

The Bible and Mystery. The Bible is very important precisely in that which we cannot readily understand. For all Christians, there are parts of the Bible that speak to us, and parts that have not yet done so; but if its entire contents were immediately relevant and meaningful, it would not be the Word of God. St. Paul exclaims before the mystery of God: 'O the depth of the riches and wisdom and knowledge of God! How unsearchable are his judgments and how inscrutable his ways!' (Rom. 11:33).

The reading of the entire Word of God (as well as the observance of the whole liturgical year) is essential for our total exposure to the mystery of God. There will be that which we thought we understood and in which we now find new and unsuspected depths; there will be that which made no sense, and that which we had not noticed, in which meaning is now revealed.

There will be aspects for which we are not yet ready, either personally or as a community; there will be aspects that are more important for other generations in the Church's history than our own. We have to be open to the entirety of the Word, and firmly to resist the temptation to write off, ignore and excise from our theology that which is not immediately meaningful. 'If it doesn't make sense, chuck it out' is as good advice as can be imagined for the emasculation and debilitation of Christian life.

Our task is to be open and to listen; if we do this, there is no need to be anxious when parts of the Scriptures do not make immediate sense. For the Lord will lead us when it is time; he is the revealer, and it is by his Spirit that our eyes are opened to what he is saying.

Hard Sayings. Besides those parts of the Bible that do not as yet speak to us, there are other passages which we do understand but which we do not like, at least at first hearing. These are those teachings and episodes which present us with the same challenge as that experienced by the disciples after Our Lord's discourse on the bread of life. 'Many of his disciples, when they heard it, said "This is a hard saying; who can listen to it?" But Jesus, knowing in himself that his disciples murmured at it, said to them, "Do you take offence at this? . . . the words that I have spoken to you are spirit and life." ' (John 6:60-61, 63).

All of us have our weak points, the areas in ourselves that need to be healed: and the Word of God is going to touch these sore spots. That is how they are healed. There is a danger here of our keeping to our favourite spiritual guides, who say the things we want to hear, and who keep well away from our weak points. This is why there is no substitute for the Bible in facing us with all the dimensions of the call to wholeness. We need to hear the hard sayings, for despite our fears, they are truly spirit and life.

St. Paul says the same thing to the Corinthians, and shows how our blind spots regularly centre on suffering and the Cross. 'For Jews demand signs and Greeks seek wisdom, but we preach Christ crucified, a stumbling block to Jews and folly to Gentiles' (1 Cor. 1:22-23). That the Christian life means taking up the Cross of Christ and following him along the road of sacrifice is not what either Jew or Greek want to hear; it is a hard saying, but St. Paul continues 'to those who are called both Jews and Greeks, Christ (is) the power of God and the wisdom of God' (1:24), 'For the word of the cross is folly to those who are perishing, but to us who are being saved it is the power of God' (1:18).

We need to hear the hard sayings of the Gospel, if we are to hear what God is saying through the hardships and calamities of life. But if we do not feel that combination of fear and of hope when the Gospel is read, we are unlikely ever to receive the initially unwelcome and threatening. The hard sayings carry hope, for that is why they are spirit and life; so when the Word cuts to the heart, it heals and restores. God's judging Word is a saving Word.

There is a vast gulf between allowing ourselves to speak the hard saying of the Gospel and intending to preach a hard word with relish, socking it to the congregation! Such sadistic behaviour in the pulpit carries no hope, builds nothing, and is never from the Lord; for the hard saying is always the absolute character of the Gospel striking home, like the rich young man hearing the invitation of Jesus. The Christian preacher knows that he must not water it down, knows that some will find it hard, but he speaks with love, and like Jesus is sorrowful over those who turn away.

Biblical Imagery. The Bible not only provides us with ideas and with teaching, but also with images, with parables and with poetry. Soaking ourselves in the Bible serves as a powerful corrective to the view that regards imagery as something to be transcended, and as only appropriate to the earlier stages of prayer. This mistake is the spiritual version of the theological attitude that parables and poetry are only containers for idea-content, to be thrown away as soon as the theology is distilled therefrom.

The constant pattern of imagery and of visionary experience in the lives of the saints reminds us that the road to holiness does not lead out of and above all images and concepts. Thus the most spiritual of the Gospels, that of St. John, is far from being the most image-free; and indeed it is the most symbolic of the four.

What does happen as we grow in prayer is that the role of imagery changes. At the start, the use of our imagination is necessary to move the will to motivate us to hear the Word of God, and to open to him. The imagination then serves to prepare us for prayer, to bring us to the point at which the heart starts to respond, and prayer proper begins. As we become more conformed to Christ, this preparation becomes unnecessary, and our prayer becomes more continuous, starting readily enough whenever we turn to God (and in a way is going on before we consciously turn to God and tune in to him). By this time the role of imagery and of parables has changed, and their place is likely to come later in the process. It is likely then that the silence of personal non-conceptual communing with God is filled, rather than interrupted, by pictures, visual images and potential parables, that are one with our prayer. They may be images that teach us (as in many biblical visions), or they may have no discernible meaning. But they can still be part of our spiritual nourishment even without the mind being consciously enriched.

The Bible shows us how symbolic human actions common to whole cultures and to all peoples have been taken up and associated with particular events in the history of salvation. The biblical images and symbols are means by which we enter into our human and cultural inheritance, and into the mystery of Christ. This is of particular importance in our day, when we are bombarded by a succession of images and audio-visual stimuli, not all of which are obviously conveying Christian values. Our answer cannot just be a flight into a silent world without adverts or transistors, but must involve a creative encounter between the Scriptural imagery and that which is prevalent in our day.

The Bible is an important safeguard against the wrong sort of silence enveloping our prayer. It prevents our silence becoming a self-contained world, of me perfecting myself in flight from a contaminating world. The Word of God ensures that our silences are silences with the Lord, and not just silences on our own. Reading and hearing the Word accustoms us to listening, to allowing the divine Word to be born within our silence, that we become fruitful not sterile. If we are hearers of the Word, we need not worry whether our times of silent wordless concept-free prayer might really be empty day-dreaming; this is an anxiety promoted by the evil one to send us back to the busyness of saying prayers. 'The Word of God is living and active, sharper than any two-edged sword, piercing to the division of soul and spirit, of joints and marrow ... discerning the thoughts and intentions of the heart' (Heb. 4:12); this piercing to the heart, that is the repentance already mentioned, is a sign that our silences are with the Lord. They then deepen the word that has been received, as with Our Lady, who kept all these things in her heart; Mary is the typical hearer of the Word, and the type of the contemplative.

The Word not biblical themes. In these days, when people often look for one theme in the readings at Mass, and want themes to use in prayer groups, it needs to be said that no one passage of Scripture only contains one theme. We have to hear the Word of God, not biblical themes distilled by some well-meaning commentator.

Times of prayer, whether liturgical or extra-liturgical, whether public or private, need to include some hearing of the Word, which then allows the hearers to respond as the Spirit of God touches them. For no passage of Scripture is so confined that it can only spark off prayer in one determined direction. Readings are starting-points for prayer; the Word is a seed, and we must let it come up and flourish where the Lord sows and where the Lord gives increase.

Within the liturgy, this prayer-provoking capacity of Scripture can be fostered by encouraging times of silence after the Scripture readings, and by a more reflective use of the responsorial psalm and alleluia verse. We will then rediscover the rhythm of the Word of God and the word of prayer, and of the role of music in a communal prayer-response; at present this rhythm is sadly lacking at most liturgies, with the responsorial psalm and alleluia verse just being part of one continuous reading from after the collect to the end of the Gospel.

Within prayer-groups, greater flexibility is possible, but rules about use of the Bible are not desirable. This is a situation in which the rich potential of Scripture to inspire a wide range of prayerful response is often made manifest; and a creative juxtaposition of Scriptural imagery and personal prayer can result. The temptation should be resisted to use Bible passages to predetermine the course of prayer; when the occasion naturally suggests a particular theme (e.g. in Holy Week, after a local tragedy, on the eve of an ordination or a marriage), a suitable biblical passage will readily come to someone's mind and the depth of sharing rather than the use of Scripture will determine whether the theme remains or varies. Sometimes, suitable passages will be suggested to one person by the prayer of another; what is helpful is always to have a Bible at hand.

In our private prayer, the Bible should also have a prominent place. More need not be said as to how; some people need more organisation, and may be well-advised to develop a fixed pattern of bible-reading; others need less organising and can achieve the same results in a less systematic manner.

The Bible and weakness in prayer. Some of our difficulties in praying flow from the lack of a biblical basis, and a weakness in regard to some of the aspects of prayer noted in this chapter. This concerns how familiar we are with the Scriptures and how much we have made our own the New Testament pattern of prayer (as in the Name of Christ, as eschatological, as work of the Spirit) and have imbibed its richness of wisdom and imagery.

In this age of great advances in biblical exegesis, the danger has arisen of biblical texts being used for prayer only in a literal or an exegetically scientific way, the fundamentalist of course restricting himself to the former. As a result, various ways in which the Church has used the Bible, the allegorical and spiritual senses of Scripture, and the creativity of the liturgical juxtaposition of texts, have been forgotten. Poetry has been replaced by science, and this has accentuated the process already under way of the intellectualisation of our prayer, so that prayer has become 'holy thinking', a dealing with ideas rather than the living God.

Sharing in Prayer

It has become a commonplace in modern Catholic theology that the Christian community is gathered and formed in response to the Word of God. What have not been so commonplace are the consequences for all our prayer that flow from this understanding of the Church.

The Christian community that is the Church is actualised in faith and worship: sharing in prayer is part of what it means to be the Church, for Christianity focuses on sharing and on praying. Thus praying with others is not an optional extra for those Christians who find it helpful; it is the natural consequence of being given the same Spirit within the one body of Jesus Christ.

It is necessary to state this theology of the Church as worshipping community in order to start from a truly Christian model for understanding our prayer, as well as providing the proper context for discussing liturgical prayer, group prayer and other forms of sharing in prayer with fellow-believers.

Any act of prayer is normally accompanied by at least an implicit model for understanding prayer; and it is clear from the attitudes of many Christians to praying with others that this model is frequently that of a one-to-one communication, viz. me and God. Such a model will influence what we do whenever we try to pray.

The theology of the Church as worshipping community means that the only proper model for understanding our prayer is that of the Church, the communion of those who are going to the Father through and in Jesus Christ. Whether we pray on our own or with others, we pray as members of the body of Christ; this community-context of all our prayer does not only affect the content of our prayer (e.g. whether we intercede for others in the Church, whether we speak in the singular or in the plural) but also the very way we pray, for we learn to pray within the Church. Our very individualism is part of an ecclesial inheritance!

Teaching people to pray cannot help but be a community activity. The word of God which provokes the response of prayer is uttered in community, and the Bible is the book of the Church. The prayers we are taught are part of a spiritual inheritance. So when we start to pray, we do so by entering, however imperfectly, into a spiritual tradition, and a heritage of prayer. And even where there are no customs of praying spontaneously with others, we still learn by seeing others pray, by taking in what it means to them, by copying their devotional practices, as well as the learning that takes place within the liturgy.

But most importantly, all prayer is a gift of God in Christ. This is true not only of the general possibility of praying (that we can only pray at all because God enables us to do so), but also of each particular prayer that is prayed. As with all God's gifts to his People, prayer is given within the Body of Christ, and needs to be understood in the context of St. Paul's teaching on the charismata being organically inter-related in the Body of Christ. 'Now there are varieties of gifts, but the same Spirit; and there are varieties of service, but the same Lord; and there are varieties of working, but it is the same God who inspires them all in every one. To each is given the manifestation of the Spirit for the common good' (1 Cor. 12:4–7).

This means, first, that all prayer is complementary to that of our fellow-believers; the prayers we are given are conditioned in their giving by the prayers God is giving to others.

Thus even when I pray on my own, what God is doing in me is linked with what he is doing in others; I may not know how, but God does. Secondly, God's gift of prayer to me is not only for my own benefit, but is also for the sake of others; and this does not only apply to the prayer of intercession.

These thoughts show that all Christian prayer should be made with our model for prayer being the Church; the ideal is to pray in the consciousness of being part of the praying Body of Christ. Sharing in prayer then calls for a shared awareness of God, and of our praying to him in Christ; this awareness does not follow automatically from community worship, for this may mean anything from a mere synchronising of private praying to a common consciousness of addressing the Father in the Spirit. The former is hard to transcend when Church members are strongly imbued with the one-to-one model of prayer.

Despite our uninterrupted liturgical tradition, we have to learn to pray as members of the Body of Christ. We have to reverse the historical process by which Western man's consciousness of God, his spiritual life and his prayer-world have become essentially private; so that, as a result, his only ventures into the public forum have been governed by closely prescribed conventions (e.g. in the liturgy and in spiritual direction), within which the private categories and consciousness of the spiritual life have still operated. Recent liturgical reforms (altars facing the people, priests looking at those they address, the Pax, the singing of hymns during and after communion) are steps in the direction of 'deprivatisation', but have barely begun to tackle the underlying problem, our privatised consciousness of God.

A shared awareness of God involves a common focus among those praying together, with a background awareness of our fellow-worshippers doing the same thing. When we pray with others, our attention must be on the Lord, not on those with whom we are praying. But this does not mean that we should attempt to exclude these others from our consciousness, and they will normally remain within our conscious horizon. This is surely what is meant in Acts when we are told that 'the company of those who believed were of one heart and soul' (4:32). Much damage has been done by a swing from a private focus on God to a horizontal focus on our fellow-worshippers as being 'in Christ'. This may appear to be a promotion of Christian charity, but it is in fact a firm step away from real prayer. That such a switch has not had more disastrous results is due to the fortunate fact that the liturgical texts express something quite other than this horizontalism.

Sharing in prayer is then much wider than 'shared prayer' or 'group prayer', wider indeed than liturgical prayer. Without this wider context, which is the Church understood and lived as a praying people, all our talk about liturgical prayer, shared prayer, and private prayer is likely to be lop-sided. There is an important sense in which there are no such things as liturgical prayer, shared prayer and private prayer; there is just prayer. And the adjectives—liturgical, shared and private—are describing somewhat incidental features of this basic activity called prayer, namely whether we are using approved formulae, following determined rites, whether we are praying more informally with others, or whether we are on our own. Thus anything we learn about prayer from one form of praying applies to all forms of praying; for all learning about prayer is really coming to know and love God. Praying with other people also teaches us about love, for we come to know them as being in Christ, and to accept them as our brothers.

All prayer involves the turning of our hearts and minds to the Father in Christ—whether we are with others or not, whether we are using words or not, whether we are standing, kneeling or sitting. The model of the Church as God's praying people, as the worshipping Body of Christ, as the Temple of the Holy Spirit, provides the means for integrating our experience and understanding of different forms of praying, so that the unity of all prayer is not just affirmed in theory but lived in practice.

However the fact must be faced that most of us start from a situation in which liturgy and private prayer are not experienced as one. This lack of integration may show up in any one of three ways: (i) by giving the priority to private prayer, adopting the *solus cum solo* model for all prayer, subordinating liturgical prayer to this pattern and thus praying privately during the liturgy, regarding others as potential distractions; (ii) by treating the liturgy as self-sufficient, and devaluing private prayer, perhaps emphasising the horizontal element in the liturgy making others the focus of attention and thereby reducing God to an atmospheric element; and (iii) by valuing both, but operating on two different models and failing to achieve synthesis and integration; this kind of division leads to some things being valued in liturgy, e.g. fixed formulae, ordered celebration, prescribed postures, and quite different things in private prayer, e.g. spontaneity and silence, without any lessons being learned from one for the other.

The gap between the two is evident in the sphere of formation and education. When we teach people about liturgy, we do not readily think of this as helping them to pray; and when we speak in the pulpit or in schools about prayer, it means first and foremost private prayer, rarely what we do in the liturgy.

Numerous writers in recent years have deplored this gap between the liturgy and private prayer, but all too often what is offered is a mere intellectual relating of each to the other, the production of a theory about their relatedness. It is one of the great blessings of group prayer that it helps to bridge this gap existentially: for group prayer, or perhaps better shared prayer, is similar to liturgy in that it is prayer with others, and it is similar to private prayer in that we are free to pray in set words, our own words, or no words.

We are now in a position to consider in turn the respective

values, role and potential of liturgical prayer, shared prayer, and the other ways in which we share in prayer.

Liturgical Prayer. One aspect of the gap between the liturgy and private prayer is right and inevitable, at least in the earlier stages; for the liturgy is that into which we have to grow.

The liturgy reflects the moods and sentiments of the Church Catholic, of the redeemed People of God; whereas frequently private prayer reflects the little world of me and my needs. To experience the liturgy as our own prayer can only happen when we truly enter into the mystery of the Church, and when we are radically open to the Spirit of God that animates the Church. We have to be called out of our little world, with ourselves at the centre, into the real world of redeemed creation, centred in Jesus Christ.

Spiritual growth will lead to an increasing love for the liturgy; the Holy Spirit works to raise us to the level of the liturgy, which is the prayer of Jesus Christ to the Father. The greater our identity with Jesus Christ, the greater will be our affinity with the liturgy. So we are led from an earlier stage of trying during the liturgy to concentrate on the meaning of words, that are out there, somehow above us, to the point at which these are the words we really want to say, when the language of the liturgy is found within the heart. When we reach this point and our hearts are filled with praise and thanksgiving, we discover with some surprise how much praise and thanksgiving there is in the liturgy and phrases we have said for years suddenly come alive and burst with new meaning.

The liturgy gives the rest of our prayer its proper context. Private prayer, and indeed group prayer, can sometimes be presented as if it arises in a vacuum—here am I, wanting to pray, starting from scratch, so off I go, getting rid of distractions, fixing my desire on the Lord, etc., as though I am the first person ever to pray. This impression can be given, unintentionally perhaps, when we emphasise, rightly, the need to come to prayer with open hearts and open hands, ready to go where God leads.

But, of course, God is not working in a vacuum; he has sent his Son, and poured out his Spirit. He has given gifts to men in every generation; in the words of one of the new eucharistic prayers 'From age to age you gather a people to yourself, so that from east to west a perfect offering may be made to the glory of your name.' And as the saints sing of the Lamb 'by thy blood didst ransom men for God from every tribe and tongue and people and nation' (Rev. 5:9).

Through the prayer of the liturgy, we enter into a history of praise and worship and realise our historical moment as given within a greater whole; the liturgy gives context and structure. It shows Christian prayer as within the trinitarian framework, as within an eschatological setting, and as combining praise, thanksgiving, intercession and contrition. So the given-ness of our personal prayer occurs within the givenness of the Incarnation, of Pentecost, and of all the history of salvation.

This structure of liturgical prayer is not a structure of technique, but a structure of life. That is to say, the framework of the liturgy is not in any sense an effective way of organising things; its structure is not that of a proven and tested formula, as though this way it really works. Its structure is that of the life of faith, and of the life of God, into which we are drawn by faith. So it shows in its make-up man responding to the Word of God, man receiving gifts from his Creator, above all receiving the gift of God's own Son, and thanking the Father through that Son Jesus Christ. The Spirit is then part of that structure, paradoxical though it may seem to link Spirit with structure, for the Spirit is the Spirit of the Son as of the Father, and by the Spirit the humanity of Jesus is formed.

In this respect the liturgy provides a yardstick for our personal prayer, e.g. whether or not the latter has a similarity of trinitarian and eschatological pattern to the liturgy, whether or not it has a similar blend of praise and petition, of thanksgiving and penitence. Such a testing role for the liturgy does not mean constantly analysing the components of our personal prayer, but it does provide, particularly for spiritual guides and counsellors, an important criterion for discerning how a person's prayer is developing.

Fixed and Free. The fixed aspect of the liturgy reminds us that in all prayer, we are being drawn into something far bigger than ourselves, namely the paschal mystery of Christ. It is one of the weaknesses of home-made acts of worship that for all their sincerity and informality they may fail to rise above the limitations of their authors. With the liturgy, the authors are countless generations of believers, and so we enter into the richness of this catholic unity. In this respect, liturgy and personal prayer are complementary; the liturgy should guarantee the fullness and the Christian life-structure, whilst the personal promotes the sincerity and authenticity.

Their complementarity shows that it is a mistake to contrast too sharply the structured form of liturgical prayer with the unstructured patterns of private prayer; for it is wrong to assume that the liturgy is entirely fixed, and that private prayer is wholly spontaneous. The more rigid forms of Catholic liturgy prior to Vatican II may have made easy such a conclusion; but that devalues the proper element of spontaneity and creativity in the liturgy, and overlooks the traditional aspect of private prayer. Much less should such a contrast be used to suggest that liturgical prayer is more suited to those who need rules and organisation, and that private prayer is the thing for the more independent and enterprising.

This book is not the place to debate what makes prayer liturgical, though it should be noted that our clear distinction between liturgical and non-liturgical did not exist in the apostolic Church (which is not to say that no basis for it can be there discerned) and that our present understanding of this distinction is more canonical than has generally been recognised, being the result of close ecclesiastical control of official forms of prayer, a control which clearly can only extend to official acts of the gathered community.

All living is a combination of tradition and creativity, of creativity within tradition; and this is true of all forms of prayer. But precisely because the liturgy is always both communal and catholic, and is an expression of the Church, the creativity that is appropriate is more that of whole communities, indeed of generations, of regions and cultures, of entire societies. What is objectionable about much unauthorised liturgical innovation is not so much the infiltration of creativity where it has no place, but the idiosyncratic and private character of such initiatives, resulting in the infliction of personal whims and theories on whole communities.

Much can be learned about creativity in worship from group prayer situations; and it is a regular hazard of liturgical reform that it stems more easily from compromises in committee than from the experience of communal prayer. There is in fact an element of adaptation in every liturgical celebration, a point that is more obvious the wider our experience of spontaneous corporate prayer. To consider only the celebrant, the way he holds his hands, the inflections in his voice, the points at which he pauses, where he is looking and when, are all forms of adaptation, whether or not done by conscious choice. The right forms of adaptation are discovered within the praying, and are given with entry into that prayer; the wrong way is prior to prayer or without praying to select the right pose, the right volume level, the right place to look. Creativity in worship must be the creativity of worship, that arises within the worshipping; this is not a counsel against advance preparation, but a reminder that the basic preparation is in previous prayer.

The Language of Prayer. Between liturgical and non-liturgical prayer, there is the ordinary relationship between learning a language and using that language creatively. The language of the liturgy includes that aspect of a world we enter, a culture we inherit, an inheritance we receive. At the heart of this inheritance is the Bible, a point which highlights the importance of the quality of biblical translations.

These points are of prime significance for our growth in prayer. For our prayer-language involves a naming of God, and a narrating of his deeds. Progress in the Christian life involves a steady dethroning of the idols we substitute for the living God; we have an inbuilt tendency to try to reduce God to our own size and measure, seeking to control and manipulate him. In the sphere of language, this tendency shows up in every attempt to frame technically correct formulae, and in the reduction of symbolic open language to closed technical terminology.

The language of the liturgy here provides a model for our private praying: so that our personal prayer is expressed in the rich liturgical and biblical terms, so full of allusions, open to unlimited meaning, resonant with the poetry of the spirit. The psalms manifest this quality, being like all poetry a spacious land we can enter and inhabit, however varied our situations and our needs; and growth of the human spirit involves learning the language of praise, of glory, of thanksgiving and of blessing, resisting every temptation to reduce the meaning of biblical and liturgical words to clear-cut definable tools. The breadth of our prayer-language is directly related to the possibilities for spiritual enlargement and progress.

Shared Prayer. Since we pray as members of the Body of Christ, and in our praying strengthen and comfort one another, it is natural to look for opportunities of praying together besides the official liturgical actions of the Church.

It is natural that we should pray with those with whom we share a common task or a common concern—that priests who work together pray together, that a family anxious over one member should express this concern together in prayer, that those who have been blessed corporately should thank God corporately. This is in fact the pattern we find in the Acts of the Apostles: e.g. 4:24-31 (prayer on the release of Peter and John), 10:44-48 (the coming of the Holy Spirit on the family of Cornelius), 12:5, 12 (prayer of the community for Peter in prison), 16:25 (Paul and Silas in prison), 20:36 (Paul with the elders at Ephesus), 21:5 (Paul at Tyre). And we are told that groups of Christians 'gave glory to God' (Acts 11:18; 21:20).

Sharing in prayer with our fellow Christians is fundamental in the Christian life, flowing from the nature of the Church. Praying with others apart from the liturgy should also be natural, for the liturgy on its own does not allow sufficient time and space (and cannot be celebrated anywhere on the instant). But the form taken by this sharing can be as varied as the patterns in our private prayer, indeed more so varying as much as the varieties between people and the meetings of people. Regular prayer-groups or prayer-meetings are only one way, though perhaps a particularly helpful and ordered way, of sharing spontaneously in prayer. Whether it is right for me to join a prayer-group, and if so, which one, are questions to be prayed about, and God's will sought, rather than assumptions being made about the necessity of getting as many people as possible into prayer-groups.

The question with whom we pray is closely linked with whom we live, work and otherwise share. There is something odd if people rush round the country to countless prayer-meetings and do not pray with their own base community; though God may help us powerfully in some other place, so that we can face up to and play our part in renewing the life of our own community.

One of the great hazards in the life of prayer-groups is the worship of technique. We seem to have an inner compulsion to work out theories and to elaborate techniques: a 'how to do it', 'how to run a prayer-group kit'. Resisting this temptation is the lifelong task of letting God be God, of letting Jesus be our Lord, of letting the Spirit blow where he will. Every technique we introduce limits and cramps the Spirit.

We introduce a technique whenever we work out right ways of running a prayer-group: the right way to start, the right way to finish, the ideal size for a group, whether a group needs a leader, the right ingredients for a meeting (how much silence, how much singing, how much intercession), how to deal with particular problems and producing standard solutions (speaking to people afterwards, taking them out of the meeting, 'praying over' them, exorcising them). We introduce technique when, whether consciously or not, we adopt criteria for success other than doing the Will of God: whether the numbers go up, whether anybody prays in tongues, whether the mood is joyful, whether an identifiably new gift of the Spirit is experienced.

It is easy to see how all this happens; indeed, we should expect it to happen, but expect too that we grow out of it with the help of God. For a common pattern is that when we first have a positive experience in a prayer-group, or when we overcome some difficulty, we assume that this is the way for everyone else and we erect our experience into a general rule. Now, the Lord may lead some others that same way, but almost certainly he will lead some in other ways. This is a measure of God's greatness and of the height of his ways over our ways (cf. Is. 55:9); and all our ways of doing things when turned into techniques limit the action of God, however zealous and missionary our intentions may be.

It is God we must speak of, not man-made systems; and it is prayer we must promote, not just our ways of spreading it. In all the instances given above, the introduction of techniques and rules is a substitute for discerning the Will of God: how to start, how to end, how to cope with this problem, whether anyone is to lead—on all these and other points we must pray and seek the guidance of the Lord.

The only rules that can be rightly produced are those of what it is to be Christian—the rules of love, of honesty, of freedom, of faith. And the only essential structure is the structure of Christian life, flowing from the structure of God: of the Father sending his Son, speaking his Word through the action of the Spirit, and drawing all back through the Son to the Father. This is the structure already noted in the liturgy, that of Word and response, of gift and thanksgiving, of faith, hope and charity.

Any other techniques are attempts to manipulate God, and so to bring him in some way under our control. They are looking for security and success in the wrong place—in human systems rather than in the Lord. The warning 'technique cramps the Spirit' does not rule out the giving of advice. So we can say to groups that are starting: it is helpful to fix a definite length of meeting (otherwise most of the time will be spent wondering how long it will go on), it is helpful to start with a passage from Scripture, to have a recognisable concluding prayer, etc. But these are tips, not rules; and as soon as we turn tips into fixed rules, we are erecting our idols, so that what was once a helpful tip becomes an unhelpful rule, restricting the development of our prayer.

Numbers is a point on which the technique temptation is particularly strong: for we may think we should apply principles about optimum numbers from group dynamics to prayer-groups. Whilst clearly aspects of group behaviour are found in prayer-groups, for they are human gatherings, a straightforward application is misleading. For the purpose of prayer-groups is different from other groups, and this difference grounds other variable factors: the difference in addressee (i.e. God rather than other members of the group), the different significance of silence, and a different notion of participation (the silent member of a prayer-group may have a quite different role and significance from silent members in sensitivity groups). With numbers, as with everything else, we must pray. If we feel a group is getting too big, we must pray about it peacefully, trusting the Lord, being somewhat suspicious of ready-made solutions such as 'when you reach a certain figure, split in two'. If we regularly pray about possible changes, we will find that we rarely end up by doing exactly what we thought of doing before we prayed.

Pomposity and solemnity should be avoided in the establishment of prayer-groups. Prayer is what matters; and a group serves the Kingdom of God if it prays, and the more so the deeper it prays. But a prayer-group is never the beginning of Christian prayer in a district, and we should not begin a group as though the Holy Spirit is a newcomer in our locality. It is important too not to cross-question visitors and first-timers for their reactions after the meeting; some people may need time to come to terms with their experience, and a forcing of issues is often premature. In any case, such questions rarely serve the needs of those questioned, and more often reflect anxieties in the questioners.

Likewise the blend of silence, speech and song cannot be determined in advance. Again tips can be given, e.g. if there is very little silence, that is not a good sign, and may mean you are not listening to the Lord. But you cannot apply such a criterion automatically to a single meeting. We cannot even say that spiritual progress will lead a group to sing more or to say less: all we can say is that the more we grow in the Lord, the more we will be responsive to his Spirit, be doing his work, and the more we will be abounding in praise and thanksgiving.

Other Forms of Sharing. It is important to realise that by virtue of what we are, we either strengthen or weaken the faith of those we meet; we do this by the way we live and the way we pray. A person praying fervently in church and in deep communion with God communicates something of this to others in the building, especially to others trying to pray. Likewise with a priest saying his office, and with all prayer before others.

There are other forms of praying together with which Catholics have long been familiar: a priest praying the prayers of the Ritual with a sick or dying man, religious or clergy saying the Rosary together, various forms of devotion, jointly making the sign of the Cross, saying grace before meals.

All these instances remind us that sharing prayer in small groups is not so unfamiliar as we might think. But the more we develop this praying and the freer and more open to the Spirit it becomes, the more will we carry back a heightened 'shared awareness' into these other situations.

One immediate result of sharing in prayer is that the gap between our 'spiritual' lives and our 'real' lives begins to disappear. Our life with God, our life of prayer, becomes open to other people in the same way as all our other human activities. By this, I do not mean that each one bares his soul to all and sundry at the slightest provocation, but that prayer becomes subject to the same conditions of human interaction as all our 'non-religious' activities. Just as we share some interests only with a few close friends, and other concerns with many, so too in prayer we reveal more of ourselves to a few, and rather less to many others. There is an absolute parity in this respect with ordinary human converse.

This parity applies too in regard to growth and correction. In each part of our lives, it is the public dimension, and our openness to others, that makes possible progress and mutual correction. We learn through our interaction with others, to whom we give and from whom we receive; in isolation we cannot grow. The spread of conscious sharing in prayer therefore offers great hope of mutual help and upbuilding in the life of the Spirit.

Praying With Faith

Prayer is the characteristic act of faith. You cannot live by faith without praying. Jesus Christ is praying, and by our faith in him he prays through us. To be in Christ is to be a praying person.

Praying with Confidence. In the Mass, we are invited 'Let us pray with confidence to the Father'. We can pray with confidence because Jesus is the Lord, whose prayer is of the Father and is accepted by the Father. We can pray with confidence because we are in Christ; because the Gospel has come to us 'not only in word, but also in power and in the Holy Spirit and with full conviction' (1 Thess. 1:5).

The New Testament speaks of praying in even stronger terms than confidence: it uses the word *parresia*, or boldness. 'Since we have such a hope, we are very bold' (2 Cor. 3:12). In Ephesians we are told that in Christ 'we have boldness and confidence of access through our faith in him' (3:12).

What is clear from the Bible is that this confidence and boldness are not based on anything in us (other than our faith), but they are rooted in God and in Jesus Christ. 'Such is the confidence that we have through Christ toward God. Not that we are competent of ourselves to claim anything as coming from us; our competence is from God' (2 Cor. 3:4–5). It has nothing in common with being self-assured, neither with the confidence of the self-reliant nor the boldness of the brash.

The difference between the proud and the humble is not that the former is confident and the latter is not; but rather that the confidence of the proud is in himself, and that of the humble is in God. Thus God does not encourage us to an abject self-depreciation and diffidence, but he gives us a spirit of confidence, which becomes ours but is from him. St. Paul tells Timothy 'God did not give us a spirit of timidity but a spirit of power and love and self-control' (2 Tim. 1:7).

Christian confidence is based on two main pillars: what God has already done, and especially done in the resurrection of Jesus; and the absolute faithfulness of God to what he has promised.

'Through him (Jesus Christ) you have confidence in God, who raised him from the dead and gave him glory, so that your faith and hope are in God' (1 Peter 1:21); 'since we have a great priest over the house of God, let us draw near with a true heart in full assurance of faith' (Heb. 10:21–22). Some of the implications of praying with resurrection-faith have already been mentioned in the chapter on 'Praying in Christ'.

The absolute faithfulness of God we accept in faith; but this faith is seriously threatened by sin. When we are unfaithful, and let God down, we have that feeling that things cannot be the same again, that this time we have really blotted our copy-book, and how can we ever hold our heads high again! This is how man behaves, but not how God is. The Bible constantly reminds us that man is regularly unfaithful (until we find 'the faithful witness' who is Jesus Christ), but God is ever faithful, and keeps to his promises. This, for example, is the message of Hosea, the prophet who is commanded to take back his unfaithful wife. 'I will betroth you to me in faithfulness; and you shall know the Lord' (Hosea 2:20). 'Therefore thus says the Lord: "If you return, I will restore you, and you shall stand before me. If you utter what is precious, and not what is worthless, you shall be as my mouth"' (Jer. 15:19).

St. Paul tells us that 'the gifts and the call of God are irrevocable' (Rom. 11:29). This is shown in the story of David and Bathsheba; David commits a grievous sin, for which he is punished (the child conceived in adultery dies), but the promise of God is not retracted; and indeed the line of descent to the Messiah comes through that union of David with Bathsheba. Our sins do not weaken God's fidelity; they only weaken our faith in that fidelity, making it harder for us to accept that God does still love us and want us. But, as with King David, God works out his purpose in and through the messiness of our human situations, provided we cling to him in faith. So St. Paul writes of the faithfulness of God. 'He who calls you is faithful, and he will do it' (1 Thess. 5:24. Cf. also 2 Thess. 3:3).

This confidence and boldness in prayer has many practical applications: for instance, to repetition and perseverance. Briefly, the right sort of repetition in prayer is that which flows from and expresses perseverance and constancy in faith; the wrong sort is either substituting repetition for faith ('in praying do not heap up empty phrases as the Gentiles do; for they think that they will be heard for their many words', Matt. 6:7) or repeating as though God hasn't yet heard our prayer, perhaps clinging to our prayer like a dog with a bone and not letting it go to God in faith.

The true prayer of faith is itself the work of the Lord, and a word coming from him: 'so shall my word be that goes forth from my mouth; it shall not return to me empty, but it shall accomplish that which I purpose, and prosper in the thing for which I sent it' (Is. 55:11). Once we have made a prayer in faith, with no reason for thinking that prayer to be a mistake and not from the Lord, we should hold it before him; we should be like a husband who has expressed his love for his wife—the love has been expressed, and will be expressed again, but does not need constant articulation. Trust and faith make this unnecessary, even undesirable and suspicious, and free us for other tasks.

Confidence and boldness exclude vacillation in prayer, and

what we may call 'as if' or 'on the off chance' forms of praying. We cannot exclude all conditional clauses *a priori*, but these need careful watching, for they are frequently the points at which faith seeps out, at which we hedge our bets, and try to have it both ways. 'Do I make my plans like a worldly man, ready to say Yes and No at once? As surely as God is faithful, our word to you has not been Yes and No. For the Son of God, Jesus Christ, whom we preached among you, Silvanus and Timothy and I, was not Yes and No; but in him it is always Yes' (2 Cor. 1:17-19).

The definiteness of prayer in faith flows from faith being a decisive act, and in some way a burning of our boats. This is why in the life of faith, leaving one's past is so important; setting out on a journey, selling one's possessions, taking vows for life, all express this decisive following of the Lord, and the resolve not to have it both ways. What form of decisive renunciation God asks of us will be shown in the heart and through our life-situations; any determination to up and off, to sell up, etc., without such intimation is not the response of faith, but a sign of human obstinacy and a determination to get our own way whatever the cost.

These comments are not a condemnation of the Gospel prayer 'I believe; help my unbelief' (Mark 9:24), for that is a prayer of deep faith, with the immediate recognition before Jesus of inadequacy, and accepting Jesus as healer: to recognise in ourselves remaining areas of unbelief is an illumination of the Spirit. What is not a prayer of faith is the quite different form: 'O God, if there is a God, take away my sin, if there be any sin.'

The Expectations of Faith. We all have expectations, as long as we are alive; as long as there is life, there is hope. When we pray, we all have expectations, a mixture of conscious hopes, and unconscious desires and assumptions. In this section, we see how praying in faith must mean praying with the expectations of faith.

The most obvious defect in expectation is that we expect too little. This weakness ranges from the believer who has no serious expectation of God doing anything at all to the well-intentioned but misguided devotee who regards high expectations as exceeding one's station in life, and a breach of humility.

Part of the debility of too petty expectations is a failure to realise the greatness of what God has already done, and the greatness of what we already have. This is one of the great values of the recitation in worship of the mighty deeds of God, as are found in several psalms, cf. Ps. 103–106; an element which is preserved though in less detailed form in our eucharistic prayers.

Further, we commonly assume in practice that we are the ones who are active all the time, and that God acts every now and again. Whereas the truth we discover in faith is that it is we who are the part-timers, and it is God who is always at work: 'work out your own salvation with fear and trembling; for God is at work in you, both to will and to work for his good pleasure' (Phil. 2:12–13).

At the heart of God's work is his giving of the Holy Spirit to men. 'If you, then, who are evil, know how to give good gifts to your children, how much more will the heavenly Father give the Holy Spirit to those who ask him' (Luke 11:13). The Bible uses images of lavish generosity and abundant life to describe the activity of God on man's behalf. Jesus tells us: 'He who believes in me, as the scripture has said, "Out of his heart shall flow rivers of living water"' (John 7:38).

Praying with faith means turning to the most generous of fathers with the conviction that he is pouring out his love, his own Spirit, that he is longing for our growth in the image of his own Son, that he is ever at work to bring this about. To enter the Body of Christ is to swop our petty human expectations for the expectations of God as he is realising them through and in Jesus Christ. The expectations of God are summed up in the phrase 'The Kingdom of God', and it is for the realisation of these expectations that we pray whenever we say 'Thy Kingdom come'.

It must be that at first our expectations are too small; and that progress in faith expands these expectations. Our horizons have to be stretched, and our hopes deepened; so St. Paul tells the Corinthians 'widen your hearts also' (2 Cor. 6:13), widening the range of our hopes and our love.

That we have to grow into the expectations of God can be overlooked all too easily when we come into an experience of the Spirit; our expectations of the Lord soar (thank God) and almost inevitably we make assumptions about what the Lord is doing, and how he does it. These assumptions, not always made explicit in our minds, include criteria for success which are an admixture of divine and human greatness; our human criteria for success then need purification to become those of God, as shown in Jesus Christ.

This process is evident whenever anxiety arises due to things not going as we expected; we have constantly to learn that what was wrong was what we expected. We have to discover the truth proclaimed in Isaiah: 'For my thoughts are not your thoughts, neither are your ways my ways, says the Lord. For as the heavens are higher than the earth, so are my ways higher than your ways, and my thoughts than your thoughts' (55:8–9).

This anxiety that comes from God not conforming to our theories about what he should do next can only be banished by growth in faith, by confident trust that God is faithful, even if what is happening does not look like success by any human standards. It is here that we are confronted by the mystery of the Cross: that we are brought face to face with the life of Jesus of Nazareth, which hardly conforms to anyone's idea of a success story.

Our fantasies of a royal, triumphant and painless road to

glory die very hard. And we will be severely tempted (if we take Jesus seriously) to abandon the way of the Cross for ways that seem to be more obviously successful, to create and generate our own enthusiasm, to prolong the God-given joys and wonders beyond the time of their giving. We must expect each step forward to expose the fickleness of our hearts, to uncover the gaps in our dedication; when we think we are ready to do great things for the Lord, he shows us that we are not (the Apostles all over again)!

The problem of apparently big, but only humanly big, expectations is one that prayer-groups can make more evident, but which really applies to all prayer. The difference made by the group situation is that of greater mutual influence, which can operate either for good or for ill: where God is being truly sought, where the desire is to pray, and where the focus is on doing God's Will, the sharing situation of a group can be powerfully therapeutic and supportive; it will then operate to show up our false or inadequate expectations, and God can use some to show this to others. But we have to face the possibility of a group losing its focus, and slipping from real prayer, so leading to a sharing of delusions and mistakes; this can however only happen when we turn away from the Lord, and it is the literal truth to say that the only thing that can go wrong with a prayer-group is that it stops praying.

A common example concerns our expectations regarding the moods we feel in prayer: we can assume that prayer-groups ought always to be joyful, because joy is a fruit of the Spirit. And, if it is not joyful, we may pretend we are, making anxious assertions of our joy, almost trying to convince ourselves, or we may be tempted to produce joy by means other than praying. But these are temptations to forsake the path of truth and the real, and are evasions of the real struggles, the real battles the Lord calls us to fight. So if we come to prayer depressed, without a trace of joy, we should not fret, but just pray, bringing our whole depression to the Lord, as it is. It may soon become clear that our mood is due to inward-looking, to dwelling on ourselves and our unenviable lot; and that we have to look up, to face the Lord, and let him in at the centre, and then the mood will begin to change. Or it may be that praying intensifies the pain, and that the pain we bring to prayer is already a sharing in the suffering of Christ, that it is already a loving, caring pain; and that is our prayer. In this case, assertions of joy are unreal and out of place: and the Lord is likely to give us that deeper peace, that paradoxical state of being able somehow to rejoice in our sufferings, a theme well known to St. Paul (cf. e.g. Col. 1:24).

Other false expectations, and we will probably all feel them at some stage, flow from assuming everyone has to go along the same path and from assuming that progress means bigger and better versions of what we have had already. All represent distortions of the true greatness of God and of his doings; at whatever stage we are, the words of St. Paul apply, namely that God 'is able to do far more abundantly than all that we ask or think' (Eph. 3:20).

'Protect us from all anxiety.' Anxiety and fear are two of the most crippling handicaps in the Christian life, for both shackle and inhibit living faith. To learn to pray with faith is to cast off all anxiety and fear. St. Peter exhorts us: 'Cast all your anxieties on him, for he cares about you' (1 Peter 5:7).

The injunction 'do not fear' recurs regularly throughout the Bible. It is spoken in many cases to men and women called to a particular vocation or mission: thus the Lord says to Abraham 'Fear not, Abram, I am your shield' (Gen. 15:1), to Isaac 'fear not, for I am with you and will bless you and multiply your descendants' (Gen. 26:24), to Gideon 'Peace be to you; do not fear, you shall not die' (Judges 6:23), to Jeremiah 'be not afraid of them, for I am with you to deliver you' (Jer. 1:8), to Ezekiel 'and you, son of man, be not afraid of them, nor be afraid of their words, though briers and thorns are with you and you sit upon scorpions; be not afraid of their words, nor be dismayed at their looks, for they are a rebellious house' (Eze. 2:6).

We find the same message in the calls to Zechariah, to Joseph and to Mary. 'Do not be afraid, Zechariah, for your prayer is heard, and your wife Elizabeth will bear you a son' (Luke 1:13); 'Joseph, son of David, do not fear to take Mary your wife, for that which is conceived in her is of the Holy Spirit (Matt. 1:20); 'Do not be afraid, Mary, for you have found favour with God. And behold you will conceive in your womb and bear a son, and you shall call his name Jesus' (Luke 1:30-31).

The same message is also addressed to the whole people. 'Fear not, for I have redeemed you; I have called you by name, you are mine' (Is. 43:1). 'Fear not, nor be afraid; have I not told you from of old and declared it?' (Is. 44:8). 'Fear not, for you will not be ashamed; be not confounded, for you will not be put to shame . . . for your Maker is your husband, the Lord of hosts is his name' (Is. 54:4-5). 'Fear not, O land! be glad and rejoice, for the Lord has done great things' (Joel 2:21).

God calls and gives a mission; and this can only be fulfilled in faith. The one called is told not to fear, but to trust in God who has given the call; the reasons given for trust are grounded in the action of God, past, present and future. 'Fear not, I have redeemed you', so do not fear because God *has* done it; 'fear not, for I am with you', so do not fear because the Lord *is* doing it; 'fear not, for you will not be ashamed', so do not fear, because the Lord *will* do it.

In any of these, the temptation to fear and to doubt can arise. As to the past, we may wonder whether it was really God who called us; perhaps we persuaded ourselves, or weren't we rather pushed into it? It seemed so like God at the time, but now! As the present, how can I be sure that God is really with me now? Yes, I don't doubt that he began it, but might not my sins and failures have lost God's support?

I used to feel his presence, but now I don't feel anything! And as to the future, our imaginations can really get to work (and this is where the evil one is likely to make his attack): yes, everything has gone well so far, the Lord has brought me to this point in one piece, but the future ... those black clouds on the horizon, impending changes, our health, our wealth, and a seemingly endless series of potential obstacles, threats and hazards. Once we let our imaginations run along these lines, we can become paralysed by thoughts about possible problems, most of which will never in fact arise. Jesus speaks to this situation in the Sermon on the Mount: 'do not be anxious about your life, what you shall eat or what you shall drink, nor about your body, what you shall put on. . . . And which of you by being anxious can add one cubit to his span of life? . . . But seek first his kingdom and his righteousness, and all these things shall be yours as well. Therefore do not be anxious about tomorrow, for tomorrow will be anxious for itself. Let the day's own trouble be sufficient for the day' (Matt. 6:25, 27, 33-34).

We are also given a picture of the life of faith in the story of Jesus walking on the waters and calling Peter to come to him across the waves. First of all, the very call to faith produces fear: the apostles were afraid at the sight of Jesus. 'When the disciples saw him walking on the sea, they were terrified, saying "It is a ghost". And they cried out for fear' (Matt. 14:26). But then Jesus says: 'Take heart, it is I; have no fear' (14:27). Then, once launched upon the life of faith, when we have stepped out from the apparent security of the boat on to the apparent insecurity of the waters, fear strikes again; we take our eyes off the Lord, and look at the wind and the size of the waves. 'When he saw the wind, he was afraid' (14:30) and so Peter begins to sink. And the Lord says: 'O man of little faith, why did you doubt?' (14:31).

Human trust at its deepest is shown in the life of Jesus himself. He, who has worked miracles of healing, who has taught with power and authority unlike the scribes and the pharisees, who has drawn the crowds as no other contemporary teacher, now faces the apparent failure of death, the ignominious execution of a convicted criminal, together with the desertion of his closest followers, the crowd turned against him, and the hostility of all circles of society. In human terms, this is complete failure. But Jesus still trusts his heavenly Father; and so his death is confident though agonising prayer —prayer for those putting him to death, and that prayer of complete self-oblation to God 'Father, into thy hands, I commit my spirit' (Luke 23:46).

Fears and anxieties also arise within prayer; and whatever the occasion of their appearance, they must be faced in prayer. As is natural, the fears that strike us during private prayer are those that characterise people on their own, and those that hit us during shared prayer are those that afflict people in society.

On our own, we are troubled by all the fears of loneliness. We are worried whether anybody cares for us, whether our friends and loved ones really love us, whether we have been let down by those in whom we have put our trust; we are anxious about our ability to make friends, to get out of ourselves, to meet others and to cope with future demands.

These are the worries most likely to trouble private prayer. We will be anxious as to whether God has abandoned us, whether he really hears our prayers, whether our sins have cut off his love; it is at such times that the psalm prayed by Jesus in his dereliction readily becomes our prayer 'My God, my God, why hast thou forsaken me? Why art thou so far from helping me, from the words of my groaning? O my God, I cry by day, but thou dost not answer; and by night, but find no rest' (Ps. 22:1-2).

The answer must lie in trust and thanksgiving, and a speaking of our real minds to the Lord, bringing it out as did the psalmist. 'How long, O Lord? Wilt thou forget me for ever? How long wilt thou hide thy face from me? How long must I bear pain in my soul, and have sorrow in my heart all the day? How long shall my enemy be exalted over me?' (Ps. 13:1–2).

A different range of fears and anxieties afflict us in company. We experience a need to prove ourselves, to be thought well of and to make a good impression, to say the right thing, not to look a fool; we are anxious as to what others are thinking, and we don't want to be the odd one out. So comes the temptation to put on a mask, and act a part—a part that we feel will be more acceptable than our real selves.

These are precisely the feelings and temptations that will arise in the group prayer situation. We will want our prayer to be approved in the group, we will want to pray the right prayers making our prayers theologically correct or full of the approved terminology, we don't want to look foolish; and the temptation will be to put on a praying mask, to try to 'keep up with the praying Joneses'.

These difficulties should not daunt us; they are to be expected, for they are part of human experience. If we did not have such temptations in prayer, it would not be real; and the importance of facing them in prayer is that the prayer situation is the potentially most healing, where we bring our real selves to the Lord.

But whatever the source of fear and anxiety, we have to let it go. 'Have no anxiety about anything' (Phil. 4:6) says St. Paul; he doesn't say that we mustn't be anxious about unimportant things, but that we must not worry about anything at all. For anxiety denies the providence of God, that the Lord has the whole universe down to its tiniest detail, even to sparrows and the hairs on our heads, in his loving and healing care.

This is not so opposed, as may appear at first sight, to what psychologists tell us about the difference between constructive anxiety, that goes with potential for creative activity, and neurotic destructive anxiety that cripples and inhibits. As Christians we are invited to let our anxieties and fears go to the Lord: so that we live with the tension of faith, accepting the uncertainties that threaten, taking the risks involved in positive decision-making, in working with others, in loving others. Living by faith requires all the positive elements in 'constructive anxiety', the elements of tension and apprehension, but it adds the element of 'letting go', letting the Lord take the burden, of being freed from all inhibiting features.

We can helpfully look a bit further at risk and situations of risk, for these are the source of much anxiety. There is risk inherent in loving and in trusting; to live by faith is to accept the risks involved in living as God's son in a world of contradictions. Risk is involved in vocation and in mission; and God gives the grace to face the risks together with the vocation, as he says to St. Paul 'My grace is sufficient for you' (2 Cor. 12:9). Here we have to avoid the two extremes, both of which stem from lack of true faith in God: the over-cautious extreme, of trying in advance to exclude every possible risk, with the result that nothing really happens, either for God or against; and the over-zealous extreme, of seeking risk for risk's sake, trying to prove one's power of faith (to oneself), like the American sect whose leaders drank poison and died whilst their congregation chanted the praise of God (cf. Mark 16:18). We should not seek risks, but the kingdom of God and the doing of God's will; and within that right seeking, we accept the risks that are part of the task the Lord is truly giving—for that the grace and strength will be given.

At the heart of our fears and anxieties lie our emotions. Mention of prayer-groups, even without saying the bogy word 'Pentecostal', can raise the spectre of emotionalism with rather frightening ease. This fear of our emotions needs critical examination, and a discernment between the right place of our emotions in life and worship, and what is really wrong in 'emotionalism'.

Our emotions are part of us; our healing in Christ must include the healing of our emotions, and their integration within the whole personality. It is precisely total human experiences involving the whole person, emotions, heart, mind and will, such as unashamed repentance and fulsome praise, which are powerfully integrating. We cannot become holy, that is whole in the Lord, with a largely cerebral religion, with the head of a giant and the emotions of a pygmy!

Very often our fear of the emotions is a rationalising of our inability to cope with the emotions of others, and the demands they make. It is hard to enter a grieving situation when we are not closely touched by the bereavement; it is hard to enter a joyful celebration when we do not share the mood of the occasion. Such situations are demanding; but charity requires that we do face them when it is our responsibility, and that we do so with sympathy and honesty. To sympathise is to feel with: 'bear one another's burdens, and so fulfil the law of Christ' (Gal. 6:2).

In a praying situation, the manifestation of emotions is right when this is given with the prayer, that is when it is part of a person's response to God and of opening up to his grace. Frequently such an emotional release or 'letting go' is an essential part of such an opening up, and without it, the latter could not happen. When emotions arise within a real seeking of the Lord, and opening to him, we must be prepared to accept whatever happens, however unpleasant. Because what comes to the surface is something from within the person, things perhaps long hidden and repressed, and which need healing and integration. We must recognise that much of our dislike of such manifestations reflects our selfishness and pride; we are not too bothered if others are suffering acutely, so long as it is hidden from our sight!

It is evident from the Gospels that the ministry of Jesus was regularly accompanied by emotional outpourings, not to say, disorders. This reminder should be a salutary check to all our concern for clinically pure anaesthetised forms of worship. 'As he drew near to Jericho, a blind man was sitting by the roadside begging; and hearing a multitude going by, he inquired what this meant. They told him, "Jesus of Nazareth is passing by." And he cried, "Jesus, Son of David, have mercy on me!" And those who were in front rebuked him, telling him to be silent; but he cried out all the more . . . And Jesus stopped, and commanded him to be brought to him' (Luke 18:35–40). Most of us, I suspect, would be among those telling the blind beggar to be silent; and would later describe the episode in terms of embarrassment: 'there was an awkward moment just outside Jericho, some emotionally disturbed fellow by the roadside . . . we didn't know what to do with ourselves . . .'

What then is wrong with 'emotionalism'? The wrong lies in every form of exploitation, of the using of people's emotions to gain some other end. In the sphere of religion, where it can appear to be for God but still remains exploitation, it arises when we attempt deliberately to create an emotional atmosphere independently of prayer. This is often done for the best of motives, to help people to turn to God, to make it easier for them to let go, but if it is done of set purpose, rather than the mood coming with the prayer, it is never justifiable. It is this artificial creation of emotional atmosphere that is rightly called 'emotionalism'. When pepping up occurs, the focus has slipped from the Lord to the atmosphere of the meeting, and the whole period of worship will be subtly distorted as a result.

What safeguards are necessary? Ultimately, I think, only an abundance of holy men and women, of Christians with wisdom, love and discernment; so that in our prayer-groups and times of ministry, we have Christians who can discern what a particular emotional manifestation means, who can discern and recognise the work of God from the work of the evil one. That was how Jesus Christ met and ministered.

In troubled situations we must keep praying, not allowing what is happening to others to deflect us from prayer, but responding to their need within our praying. We must keep our focus on the Lord, and as long as that is retained nothing will go wrong; for the Lord will give his word which alone will be truly healing. It may be that a disturbed person should be prayed for, perhaps with an imposition of hands; it may be that a word of encouragement is given, or even that one phones for the doctor! The right response, whether dramatic or down to earth, whether exorcism or a cup of tea, will only be discovered by looking to the Lord in prayer.

Everything said in this chapter is in some way an elaboration of the prayer in the Roman Missal: 'Deliver us, Lord, from every evil, and grant us peace in our day. In your mercy keep us free from sin and protect us from all anxiety as we wait in joyful hope for the coming of our Saviour, Jesus Christ. For the kingdom, the power, and the glory, are yours, now and for ever.'

Growth in the Spirit

There are two dominant models for spiritual growth: the 'break-through' and the 'gradual'. The former represents the crisis-experience, the sudden irruption and invasion of the Spirit of God, the moment of crucial decision; the latter the step-by-step advance, the slowly eroding or gently filling work of the same Spirit. The dramatic crisis model is more generally associated with the less liturgical and more Evangelical forms of Christianity; whilst the gradual model is more typical of strongly liturgical communions and of those with a monastic tradition. It is important (and ecumenically important) to see these two models as complementary, rather than as opposed; and this can be illustrated from the biblical teaching on the work of the Spirit.

The wind, breeze or breath of the Spirit is the very opposite of a standardised manifestation; its work is as varied as the forms of life. Sometimes this Spirit blows strongly, sometimes softly. There is the light breeze, that slight movement of air, that brings life and freshness to God's creation; this is the Spirit coming like the breath of God. This breathing of God is found in the story of creation, 'the Spirit of God was moving over the face of the waters' (Gen. 1:2), and so Jesus 'breathed on them, and said to them, "Receive the Holy Spirit"' (John 20:22). This more gentle coming of the Lord is illustrated too in the story of Elijah in the cave, when the Lord was not in the earthquake, nor in the fire, but in 'a still small voice' (1 Kings 19:12). But the Spirit can come as a strong wind, sweeping away barriers and obstacles, uprooting the most entrenched objects: this is the image we find in Psalm 29 'The voice of the Lord makes the oaks to whirl, and strips the forests bare; and in his temple all cry, "Glory"' (29:9). It is the strong wind that blows at Pentecost: 'And suddenly a sound came from heaven like the rush of a mighty wind, and it filled all the house where they were sitting' (Acts 2:2).

A similar variety can be found in the water-imagery in the Scriptures. We find the gentle fall of rain, the dew from heaven, the watering of the seed; here the blessing of the Lord 'is like the dew of Hermon, which falls on the mountains of Zion' (Ps. 133:3). But there are also the more violent, death-dealing water-images, linked with the message of salvation: the deluge, from which Noah and his family are saved; the symbol of total immersion, being a form of burial with Christ that we might rise with him to newness of life (cf. Rom. 6:4). Important too are the images of abundance, of water bringing a burgeoning of life: the river in the vision of Ezekiel of which we are told 'everything will live where the river goes' (47:9) and the imagery of fountains and springs: 'For waters shall break forth in the wilderness, and streams in the desert; the burning sand shall become a pool, and the thirsty ground springs of water' (Is. 35:6–7). The images of abundance remind us that God gives with immeasurable richness, which is an essential perspective in relating the two models of growth.

Other growth images in the Bible are, for example, those of the seed 'the seed is the word of God' (Luke 8:11), of the talents producing more talents (Luke 19), of the house or temple in construction (Eph. 2:20–22), of the vine yielding fruit (John 15:1–7). Of these some refer more directly to personal growth (the seed and the talents), some more to the upbuilding of the community (the temple and the vine); both must be considered in a treatment of 'Growth in the Spirit'.

There is also in the Bible the image of Christian life as a journey to the mountain of God, a journey in which we are led by Jesus, the new Joshua: so we have the language of spiritual progress in terms of walking—walking 'by the Spirit' (Gal. 5:25), 'in love' (Eph. 5:2), 'in the light' (1 John 1:7). The image of running is also used: 'let us lay aside every weight, and sin which clings so closely, and let us run with perseverance the race that is set before us, looking to Jesus the pioneer and perfecter of our faith' (Heb. 12:1-2).

Finally, there is the language of childhood and of maturity used of the Christian life. To the Corinthians, St. Paul speaks as to babes: 'But I, brethren, could not address you as spiritual men, but as men of the flesh, as babes in Christ. I fed you with milk, not solid food; for you were not ready for it' (1 Cor. 3:1-2). And in the previous chapter, the apostle wrote 'Yet among the mature we do impart wisdom ... a secret and hidden wisdom of God' (2:6-7). Similar language is used in the Epistle to the Hebrews: 'You need milk, not solid food; for every one who lives on milk is unskilled in the word of righteousness, for he is a child. But solid food is for the mature, for those who have their faculties trained by practice to distinguish good from evil' (5:12-13). These images of childhood and maturity refer primarily to personal growth, though St. Paul clearly thinks of the Corinthian community as beginners; and in Ephesians, he finds in the growth of the body a simile for the Church 'Rather, speaking the truth in love, we are to grow up in every way into him who is the head, into Christ, from whom the whole body, joined and knit together by every joint with which it is supplied, when each part is working properly, makes bodily growth and upbuilds itself in love' (4:15-16).

The majority of these images point to the gradual step-by-step model of growth, likening the development of Christian life to the growth of any living organism (the human body, the seed, the vine). Most of the sudden crisis growth-points concern beginnings—setting out on the journey, laying the foundation stone, planting the vine, handing over the talents; but they are not exclusive to such starting-points. There is the pruning of the vine (cf. John 15:2), the flowering of the first fruit, the seed appearing above the ground, a new storey on the building—to expand the scriptural images!

The resulting picture of growth is that of both gradual progress and decisive break-through, the former providing the continuum between the latter, and the latter punctuating the former. Indeed, this pattern follows from the comparison with living organisms: these go through the crisis points of sickness, of adolescence, of child-birth and parturition, of sudden external threats, etc. This comparison makes clear that most of our time is spent on the step-by-step walking and inching forward; but also that the crisis-points are of crucial significance, and though perhaps relatively uncommon are of an importance far exceeding their frequency. The examples given show that decisive break-through experiences are not necessarily dramatic: the degree of drama and trauma may reflect temperament and degree of psychological maturity more than depth of spiritual transformation; to recognise this is not to deny the necessity of drama and trauma in many conversions.

The question arises as to how we know to which we are now being called: is God now asking me for a decisive break-through or for step-by-step walking onwards? This question has to be asked in regard to ourselves ('What is God now asking of me?') and in regard to those for whom we bear responsibility ('What is God now asking of them?').

Here there are two essential pre-requisites: first, that we are truly seeking the Lord; and secondly, that we are truly hearing God's Word. If we are not doing these things, the break-through to which we are being called is clear: we must turn round to face the Lord, and we must open our ears to hear the Word. In terms of the imagery of life being a march to the mount of the Lord, these deviations represent the turning off the road to follow some mirage, going up a *cul de sac*; and the call is then to return to the main road.

With all the actions of the Lord, there is a correspondence between what he is doing in the heart, and what he is saying and doing through external agencies; this is a characteristic of the divine hand, for God alone fully knows the heart and what is happening therein. Within our seeking of the Lord, and our listening for his voice, we must expect the next step to be shown in the heart, and confirmed by external signs (what we read and hear, things that happen, whom we meet, etc). And we must be highly suspicious of advisers who attempt to read these external signs without knowledge or discernment of what is being shown in the heart.

The first thing then to be said to Christians wanting to grow in the Lord is about *seeking*: we must want God, we must desire him, long for him; and if we don't, we must want to desire him, and want to seek his face. This is the constant message of the Scriptures, and of spiritual authors through the ages: the 'naked intent' of *The Cloud of Unknowing*. 'As a hart longs for flowing streams, so longs my soul for thee, O God. My soul thirsts for God, for the living God. When shall I come and behold the face of God?' (Ps. 42:1–2). 'Blessed are those whose way is blameless, who walk in the law of the Lord! Blessed are those who keep his testimonies, who seek him with their whole heart, who also do no wrong, but walk in his ways' (Ps. 119:1–3). 'Seek the Lord while he may be found, call upon him while he is near' (Is. 55:6). Our Lord sums this up when he gives as his commandment 'You shall love the Lord your God with all your heart, and with all your soul, and with all your strength, and with all your mind' (Luke 10:27). This too is the nub of the sayings in the Sermon on the Mount concerning our intentions: 'The eye is the lamp of the body. So, if your eye is sound, your whole body will be full of light; but if your eye is not sound, your whole body will be full of darkness' (Matt. 6:22-23). Likewise with the following saying 'No one can serve two masters; for either he will hate the one and love the other, or he will be devoted to the one and despise the other' (Matt. 6:24). So 'where your treasure is, there will your heart be also' (Matt. 6:21).

What then are we seeking? Where are our hearts? What is our treasure? A hearing of the Word, and a turning towards the Lord, may reveal that we have been off track, seeking other things, fabricating idols after our own image and likeness. And then the jump of repentance is indicated—externally by the Word, heard or read, internally by the action of the Spirit in the heart. In this situation, we must ensure that the Word is truly heard, that the whole person is confronted by the Word and convicted of sin (cf. John 16:8); that the repentance is complete, and not left half-done, in an indeterminate position between the world and the Lord, seeing the mess that is sin, but not yet breaking through to any point of decision, to a decisive act of faith. Often this takes time, and our ministering to those at such decisive turning-points must help the person right through to the point of decision, and not be content with just sparking off the first stirrings.

Frequently, with practising Christians, we encounter good will, a conscientious fulfilment of religious duties, a real desire to love God and to serve him, but little awareness of the role of the Holy Spirit; we find a faith based on human effort, on human good will, on human expectations. In such cases, a preaching of the Word and an attention to Christian life as described in the New Testament, will stir a desire to live more deeply by faith, to live in fact by the Spirit, in the conscious awareness of the Lord's leading; so that we live now by God's power, by his good will, with his expectations. As the Lord sows seeds in the heart, seeds of dissatisfaction with mediocrity, seeds of higher spiritual 'ambition', it is right to ask to be led into fuller life in the Spirit of God. It is here that those words of Jesus apply: 'Ask, and it will be given you; seek, and you will find; knock, and it will be opened to you. For every one who asks receives, and he who seeks finds, and to him who knocks it will be opened' (Matt. 7:7-8). And it is in the Lucan version that the words follow about the heavenly Father giving his Holy Spirit ('good things' in Matthew) to those who ask him. St. Peter describes the sequel to repentance and baptism as being the reception of the Holy Spirit (Acts 2:38).

Clearly with practising Christians, we must not talk as though they have not yet received the Holy Spirit; for as Catholics believe, the Spirit is received at baptism and at confirmation. But here we are concerned with coming to an active living by the Spirit; becoming spiritual men (cf. 1 Cor. 2:14-15), living in faith by praying without ceasing, referring all our doings to the Lord, looking for his guidance in all things.

There is often here a decisive break-through to such life in the Spirit; and ordinarily it must be sought, though there can be no standard way of seeking, no approved terminology for our asking. The only valid criterion as to the rightness of such asking is what the Spirit is giving in the heart; and we have to refrain from telling other people what we think ought to be in their hearts at any moment! But if it is given in the heart, it is wrong and foolish to discourage the asking on the grounds of pride, of getting too big for their boots, etc. Such break-throughs naturally involve an element of experience; for we can hardly be said to be living by the Spirit and walking by the Spirit, if we are never aware of the Spirit. But it is not experience that we should be seeking; it is fuller life in the Lord, living with him as Lord at the centre, and not of ourselves, of our own strength, and by our strivings.

When we do break-through to a fuller life in the Spirit, some caveats are necessary: first, that we do not make our experience the norm for everyone else, and that we do not judge the spiritual progress of others by where they come on our map; secondly, that there may well be, and probably will be, other decisive break-throughs to which the Lord will later call us. These may represent the Lord asking for an area of ourselves that we have hitherto held back, or that was not really penetrated by previous surgings of the Spirit; so we can come into a new freedom in the Spirit, and yet still not allow some part of ourselves to go through his purifying fires—our property and money, perhaps, our working situation, our hobbies. And the Lord will say: 'I want all of you, every bit.' A later growth too for priests may be a new freedom in ministry; it is common enough for priests coming into a new enthusiasm for prayer, coming to know the Lord at the centre, to be prepared by God for a new confidence in ministry, for a ministerial break-through; and this will come in the Lord's time, and again will be prepared in the heart.

Another form of crisis point is the giving by the Lord of a new vocation or mission. Here too the same principles apply: the combination of the inner working in the heart, and the outer confirmation of the call.

In all these instances, prayer is crucial; and if the Lord seems to be leading somewhere in the heart, we must pray more, and give him the space and the time. We must be prepared to wait: for waiting acknowledges that God is in charge, that he gives in his time, that he alone knows when the right moment has really come. The pregnancy image is relevant here: the time of waiting for the coming of new life, for the decisive moment of actual birth, the pain and frustration of the waiting, the longing for the hour to come. Seek and wait: we can usually manage one of these, but not both! Either we seek, and are impatient: What on earth is God doing? Why hasn't he done anything? What have we done wrong? Or we wait, without really seeking: so that we would be quite content to wait for ever without anything happening, without anyone coming. And the Lord calls us to the difficult combination: to seek and to wait.

Another crisis situation that may be revealed by the Word is one of our impotence; we feel bound, imprisoned, unable to respond. In this situation above all, we must ask the prayers of others: that those who are able, who are free, can pray for our freeing in the name of Jesus, the Lord. But in all decisive moments, we are rash to just go it alone, without advice, and most of all, without enlisting the prayer of others.

But if we hear the Word, and we are seeking the Lord, and there is no indication in the heart that a particular sacrifice is being asked, that a particular jump is necessary in faith, then we must walk purposefully, step-by-step without anxiety, without worrying whether the pace seems slow or humdrum. But we can only do this in peace, if we both seek and listen.

Discernment as to whether the Lord is pushing for a breakthrough or whether he is just asking for steady perseverance is absolutely vital. For it is easy to give disastrous advice in this matter, either way. We may, for example, tell those whom the Lord is calling to a decisive step to take things easy, to be content with a humble step-by-step advance; and this will condemn them to frustration and to immobility, for we can only truly advance where the Lord is leading. Or we may be pushing people in our eagerness, telling them they must open here and now to the Spirit in a dramatic way; and if people try this, when it is not being given in the heart, it leads to guilt-feelings ('what have I done wrong that it isn't happening to me?'), to simulation, attempting to reproduce the desired effects by human means (which is highly dangerous, for there is another agency in the business who can supply certain visible results without the Spirit). Those of us in positions of spiritual ministration and counselling need to get beyond our theories, and down to discernment: what is the Lord doing and giving? This can be the only possible way of ministering and giving sound Christian advice.

Praise and Thanksgiving

To enter more fully into the life of the Spirit is to enter a world of praise and of thanksgiving. It is to live with God truly at the centre, to live in the Lordship of Jesus Christ. This issues in praise and thanksgiving, for these forms of prayer express the truth about life: praise expresses the truth about God, and thanksgiving expresses the truth about creation and redemption.

The Prayer of Praise. 'Praise the Lord! Praise God in his sanctuary; praise him in his mighty firmament! Praise him for his mighty deeds; praise him according to his exceeding greatness!' (Ps. 150:1–2).

Praise is glorying in God because of who he is; indeed, it is more—it is entering into God's rejoicing in himself, entering into the Son's joy and happiness with the Father. In the New Testament, we find praise most fully expressed in the heavenly hymns of the Book of Revelation: there the twenty-four elders sing: 'Worthy art thou, our Lord and God, to receive glory and honour and power, for thou didst create all things, and by thy will they existed and were created' (4:11). Those who have conquered sing the song of Moses and the song of the Lamb, saying: 'Great and wonderful are thy deeds, O Lord God the Almighty! Just and true are thy ways, O King of the ages' (15:3).

Praise is by its very nature God-centred; if you are self-centred, you cannot praise, you cannot rejoice in and with another. Thanking too is not generally prominent in the selfish though it is possible to thank God much more for what he has given me than for what he has given to others, to the Church and to the world. Praise is in many respects the peak of Christian prayer, the point at which thanksgiving becomes thanking God for being God, or in the words of the *Gloria* 'We give thee thanks for thy great glory.' And once we really begin to praise, the rest of our prayer will become more God-centred: not only our thanksgiving, but also our intercession and our begging for mercy.

Because praise is just rejoicing in God, it is of no earthly use. This is not a reason for criticising it, but a reason for doing it! For many of us, life is a series of technical exercises, coping is a matter of manipulating, of doing things for ulterior motives. This tendency has been enhanced in our technological age, and so our lives become full of doing things so that something else will result. And so values like love and friendship, whose basic meaning is in themselves, and that do not exist for the sake of something else, get subtly distorted by the manipulating spirit; so that we make friends for what we get out of it. Likewise, our prayer is easily tainted by manipulation: we do this to get that—we say this prayer for that intention, and so on. Devotions may become popular, because they seem to work, i.e. to bring results. True Christian worship, however, must lead us into sheer enjoyment and celebration of God, so that all our forces, energies and hopes are gathered into the Now, to live wholly in the present moment, forgetting the past and the future, to *be* with the Lord—for no other reason than worship. In technological terms, praise is wasted time; it is not doing any evident good. But in fact it is the peak of human achievement in living the greatest of God's gifts, of entering into his own contemplation of himself; and paradoxically it will have the profoundest effects on all we do.

Ultimately the words praise and adoration express the same prayer-reality of acknowledging God to be who he is; but these two words do in fact express and convey to us different and complementary aspects. A comparison between the two can illustrate the qualities of this prayer.

The term 'praise' brings out the element of rejoicing and celebration: to open ourselves to the Lord brings joy. 'My soul magnifies the Lord, and my spirit rejoices in God my Saviour' (Luke 1:46-47).

Celebration and rejoicing are essentially activities to be shared; praise more than adoration suggests this shared communal aspect. All the images of heavenly praise depict choruses, together chanting the praises of God. The father of the prodigal son summons the whole household saying 'Let us eat and make merry; for this my son was dead and is alive again' (Luke 15:23-24). Celebrating and rejoicing on one's own is somewhat odd; this reminds us that praise in private prayer is not so much misplaced, but calls for and looks forward to community celebration.

The notion of praise also brings out more than that of adoration the work of the Spirit within the heart; that praise wells up within the human heart, so that one can speak of being filled with praise. Praise expands the human spirit, an effect suggested by the opening phrase of the *Magnificat* already quoted. 'Let the word of Christ dwell in you richly, teach and admonish one another in all wisdom, and sing psalms, and hymns and spiritual songs with thankfulness in your hearts to God' (Col. 3:16). This quotation brings out another aspect of praise, namely its natural outward expression in words, particularly in song.

Praise means making a joyful sound for the Lord, singing our Alleluias, releasing something within, something that needs to burst out to be itself. Adoration, by contrast, suggests a largely silent contemplation of the mystery of God. The complementary character of sound and silence in Christian prayer is considered separately in the next chapter.

Adoration is however not just a poor substitute for praise;

it expresses other aspects of the worship of God not so clearly conveyed by praise. Adoration expresses human prostration before the incomprehensible mystery of God; it expresses our being left breathless and speechless before his greatness. So we are told of the heavenly worshippers that they 'fall down before him who is seated on the throne and worship him who lives for ever and ever' (Rev. 4:10) and 'they fell on their faces before the throne and worshipped God' (Rev. 7:11).

We need the language of adoration as well as the language of praise. The *Gloria* of the Mass is a good example, using different terms to complete this picture of man's right posture before the Lord: 'We praise thee. We bless thee. We adore thee. We glorify thee. We give thee thanks for thy great glory.' We need all these terms, for each has its distinctive echoes, its own suggestive images; adoration without praise can lead to forgetting the Spirit within, and praise without adoration can overlook the need for total self-abasement before God.

Precisely because God is so far above our comprehension, we experience great difficulty in finding language appropriate for such worship. Silent adoration of the mystery of God is one important way of acknowledging this difficulty, and so man silently adores the inexpressible.

But God has expressed himself in his Word; and so perfect worship of the Father can be given by entering into the Word, into the only begotten Son, by entering into the prayer of Jesus Christ. So it is God coming among us, supremely so in the Incarnation, that requires and enables us to use our whole humanity, our hearts, our voices and our minds, in the worship of the Father. And so the language of praise strains human expression to breaking point; for this reason, words like Alleluia and Hosanna are important, being words to let go, to sing, even to shout, in joyful praise of the Lord. For a similar reason, the prayer of praise readily involves the piling up of titles, Lord God Almighty, Lord God of hosts, King of the Ages, etc., and the use of parallelisms so characteristic of Hebrew poetry. With the prayer of praise, language begins to play a different role, being less concerned to convey meaning to others, and becoming more a manifestation of the joy in our hearts, expressing more by the sound and style of the words than by their literal meaning, syntax and grammar.

It is at this point that the prayer of 'tongues' comes to our rescue, and makes its own kind of sense. For in an important way, it is only carrying a stage further what we have just noted about the prayer of praise—that in this prayer, and the more so the deeper it goes, language has become less a conveyor of intelligible meaning and more simply an expression of what is within, whether or not it makes great linguistic sence to the hearer. The prayer of praise is inherently extravagant—for that is what God is like!

The prayer of tongues is the Spirit activating in us in our worship of God a natural capacity for non-conceptual expression. Part of the inadequacy of our language for the praise of God is that normal human language operates through the formation of images and concepts; and when the majesty and glory of God sweep us up, our minds somehow get in the way! It is then that the prayer of tongues, which expresses the human spirit in sound and song by-passing the mediation of the mind, comes to our aid. From the nature of the case, anyone whose prayer has become predominantly the prayer of praise is near to praying in tongues; and it really is as simple as asking God for the extra push, and letting it come.

Praying in tongues is not learned and nor prepared. There are no grounds for linking it particularly with states of ecstasy and, once received, it can be begun at will, completely from cold. The only right way to understand its place in Christian worship is to treat it as prayer, and particularly as prayer of praise; much misunderstanding and confusion stem from focus on the language-aspect (any prayer of praise may not be linguistically impressive!) and from treating this phenomenon as 'extraordinary'. It is not any more extraordinary than many other operations of the Spirit of God; but it is an appropriate accompaniment to a 'second-conversion' experience, for of its nature it requires a letting go of our self-control, of our tight grip on ourselves. It is within prayer a form of dying to self and of rising to new life; beforehand, it seems folly, but afterwards it makes its own kind of sense, one might say God's sense, sense to the heart. As a miniature death-resurrection experience, it is yet another instance of the Christian pattern, of giving over more and more of ourselves to the Lord; in this way, tongues is very much a prayer of faith. In this, it follows the characteristic pattern of all prayer: so that with tongues too, there will come a time when it seems pointless, when the earlier certainty of its being the work of the Spirit seems to have gone, when we are tempted to think what we received might not have been of God at all. And here again we must keep it up, confident that the Lord was and is at work; and as with all other prayer of perseverance in faith, we will come through to further depths in our adoration and praise of God.

As a non-conceptual form of prayer, tongues help a great deal towards more total and more continuous prayer. Precisely because it does not engage the mind, we can pray in tongues when our mind is otherwise engaged (though not of course when our mouths are otherwise engaged) and when we are mentally jaded.

Another popular misconception about the prayer of tongues is that it is normally aloud and vocal. In fact, the predominant usage is *sotto voce*; and this surely is what St. Paul is saying in 1 Cor. 14:28: 'But if there is no one to interpret, let each of them keep silence in church and speak to himself and to God.' This is not an injunction against praying in tongues, but one not to do so aloud in the assembly except under certain conditions. With this goes the teaching on tongues as upbuilding the one who so prays: 'He who speaks in a tongue edifies himself' (1 Cor. 14:4) in contrast to the prophet whose prophecy edifies the church.

As with all forms of prayer, a balance is required: so with tongues must also go the prayer of ordinary language using the mind. 'For if I pray in a tongue, my spirit prays but my mind is unfruitful. What am I to do?' (1 Cor. 14:14–15). St. Paul's answer is not to abandon tongues, but to pray with the mind as well: 'I will pray with the spirit and I will pray with the mind also' (14:15). The spirit here refers to the spirit of man, not the Spirit of God. The need to pray with the spirit and with the mind is part of the need to totalise our worship, so that more and more the whole person at every level is caught up into praise of the wonder of God.

The Prayer of Thanksgiving. The Christian notion of eucharist means more than our modern 'thanks' and cannot be wholly distinguished in its biblical meaning from praise, worship and the confession of God's greatness. This can be seen from the form of the initial greetings in the epistles of St. Paul; most begin with an expression of thanksgiving (Rom. 1:8; 1 Cor. 1:4; Phil. 1:3; Col. 1:3; 1 Thess. 1:2; 2 Thess. 1:3; 2 Tim. 1:3; Philemon 4), whilst two others (2 Cor. 1:3; Eph. 1:3) begin with the blessing of God 'Blessed be the God and Father of our Lord Jesus Christ, who . . .', which is the Christian adoption of the Jewish *berakah*, a blessing which is praise of God and a thanking for whatever is expressed in the words that follow.

Today with modern languages in which praise and thanksgiving are not so closely associated, we need to examine both notions: so that we see the Christian as both a praising and a thanking person, the Christian community as a praising and thanking community.

For St. Paul the very mention of the name of God leads spontaneously into praise and thanksgiving. Writing to the early Christian communities in Greece and Asia Minor, St.

Paul remembers all God has done for them, and so he thanks. For a man so taken up with and into God as Paul, every person and situation speaks of the Lord, and is seen as his gift; every experience provides grounds for thanksgiving. For so many of us, God's creation being gift is an idea we occasionally recall; for the man of God, it is the way he lives. Every moment, every situation, every encounter is lived as gift of the Lord.

The coming of the Holy Spirit produces thanksgiving; for the Spirit shows us how things really are, namely that all has been made by God and comes from God as his gift. The coming of the Spirit opens our eyes, to see what is already there but that we did not see because of the veil over our eyes: 'when a man turns to the Lord, the veil is removed' (2 Cor. 3:16).

To have the veil removed and to live in God's world is to rejoice in the Holy Spirit and to thank. St. Luke tells us that Jesus thanked and rejoiced in the Spirit: 'In that same hour he rejoiced in the Holy Spirit and said: "I thank thee, Father, Lord of heaven and earth, that thou hast hidden these things from the wise and understanding and revealed them to babes; yea, Father, for such was thy gracious will"' (10:21).

We have to be set free to thank. As sinners, as rebellious, resentful, grumbling people, we cannot thank. We act as though we had a right to everything, we take things for granted, and so we say in our hearts 'Thank you for nothing'. To thank is to acknowledge that we are not self-sufficient, that we do depend on others, that we are the recipients of blessings not just their dispensers. But whilst thanking is not normally paramount in the self-centred, it is possible to simulate thanks as any other prayer, to learn the style (as in the prayer of the Pharisee centred entirely on himself: 'God, I thank thee that I am not like other men, extortioners, unjust, adulterers, or even like this tax collector' Luke 18:11) and it is possible for a real but imperfect thanksgiving to centre on what I have received, to thank for what I have got, what God has done for me.

Christian thanksgiving is not just a thanking for what God has done for me, or even what he has done for any particular group. The Old Testament prayers of thanksgiving thank God for the works of creation and for what he has done for his chosen people. Psalm 136 is characteristic, containing the refrain 'O give thanks to the Lord, for he is good, for his steadfast love endures for ever', then listing in litany form all the works of God, first the works of creation (vv. 5-9) and then the works of redemption (vv. 10-22). With the coming of Christ, the election of the chosen People is made fully manifest as for the sake of the redemption of all, of the whole human race and the whole cosmos. And so the great Christian act of worship, the Eucharist, is an act of thanksgiving and worship for all the works of God, of creation and redemption, for the whole human race, reaching its climax in the gift of God's only Son, Jesus Christ.

So in the Roman Mass we are invited 'Let us give thanks to the Lord our God' and we reply 'It is right and fitting'. And the celebrant takes this up in lyrical tones: 'It is truly right and fitting, always and everywhere to give you thanks, Lord, holy Father, almighty and everlasting God through your Son Jesus Christ our Lord.'

As Christians we are called to thank always and everywhere. Our thanking has to become the universal thanking of Jesus Christ, and only when we have been freed by the Spirit to live daily by his guidance will we truly experience the Mass as the great act of thanksgiving. For many of us, the Mass as thanksgiving is more a matter of theory than of experience, for we more readily experience the Mass-action in other valid but complementary terms, such as sacrifice and adoration.

St. Paul tells his hearers and readers to thank so often that one might think he was labouring the obvious. To quote a few: 'give thanks in all circumstances for this is the will of God in

Christ Jesus for you' (1 Thess. 5:18). 'He also who eats, eats in honour of the Lord, since he gives thanks to God; while he who abstains, abstains in honour of the Lord and gives thanks to God' (Rom. 14:6). 'And whatever you do, in word or deed, do everything in the name of the Lord Jesus, giving thanks to God the Father through him' (Col. 3:17). We are to abound in thanksgiving (Col. 2:7), and indeed St. Paul goes so far as to commend acts of kindness for the reason that they will give rise to greater thanksgiving! 'You will be enriched in every way for great generosity, which through us will produce thanksgiving to God; for the rendering of this service not only supplies the wants of the saints but also overflows in many thanksgivings to God' (2 Cor. 9:11-12). The apparently obvious is often the most basic and pround.

Thanksgiving and Intercession. Thanksgiving is the proper context to consider the prayer of intercession. St. Paul says: 'I urge that supplications, prayers, intercessions, and thanksgivings be made for all men' (1 Tim. 2:1). That this combination of intercession and thanksgiving is not coincidental, but stems from the nature of things is clearer in Philippians: 'Have no anxiety about anything, but in everything by prayer and supplication with thanksgiving let your requests be made known to God' (4:6).

We must thank when we ask. Our normal assumption is that we ask first, and then thank when we receive, i.e. see the prayer of thanksgiving as Christian good manners. Why then should we thank when we are asking?

First, we must thank now, because every new blessing we seek occurs within a context of past and present blessings; we are all persons who have received much, far more than we realise. To be baptised makes us thankers of the Father; we are none of us in the situation of the totally disinherited, and so we pray from this situation, saying for what we have already received, may the Lord make us truly thankful.

Secondly, it is only if we thank when asking that we are

likely to ask for the right thing! Constant thanksgiving roots us in the real situation before God, recognising what he has already done, and this makes clearer to us our real needs, and disposes us to receive what God is trying to give.

Thirdly, intercession must be a true prayer of faith, not just an assertion of self, but a submission to the Lordship of Christ. It is only when we pray in the name of Jesus that we are told we will receive that for which we ask (cf. John 14:14). But we can only pray in the name of Jesus if we thank and praise, for Jesus is the great thanker and praiser of the Father. That thanksgiving is an act of faith is perhaps less familiar than that intercession requires faith. But we only know by faith that all life is gift of the Father and it is only by faith that we believe and hold on to the truth that God has adopted us as his sons. In our dark hours, we are tempted to disbelieve, to doubt whether God has really given us his Spirit, to doubt whether we have really been forgiven. In such situations, it is not enough just to ask for the doubt to be removed; we must remove it by thanksgiving. Firm thanksgiving in faith is essential to stave off these insinuations of the evil one, that sap the very life of faith.

The level of thanksgiving is a sound test of the rightness of people's prayer and of the rightness of our intercession. It is not the size of our intercessory demands that demonstrates the depth of our faith, but the size of our thanksgiving. Indeed, it is possible for our intercession to express a lack of faith; sometimes we come across people praying for great outpourings of the Holy Spirit without any thanksgiving for what the Spirit has already done—such requests may really be saying: 'We haven't got anything worthwhile yet, but for heaven's sake give us the real thing. Just give us *that*, and then we will really have arrived.' Such thankless demanding on our part expresses a need for self-assurance, a search for security rather than faith.

Thanksgiving locates intercession within a God-centred

view of prayer. Many problems about the prayer of intercession and petition arise from seeing prayer as fundamentally man-centred, man trying to get God to do something. Thence arise hosts of false problems, such questions as whether prayer is getting God to change his mind, whether we should ask for miracles, etc. We have to abandon this man-centred view and replace it with the model of God inviting man to share in his creative activity.

St. James tells us 'the prayer of faith will save the sick man' (5:15). For the Christian, intercessory prayer is sharing in God's love and concern for that other; such a prayer is a response to God's word in our hearts (the basis of all true prayer). The prayer so uttered in faith is then instrumental in effecting the Will of God.

It is misleading to imagine prayers of petition piling up in a heavenly sorting-office, with God deciding which to accept and which to decline: as though some heavenly returning officer could finally announce the figures: 300 petitions, 175 granted, 125 refused. It is wrong to pray 'any old' prayers of petition leaving God to sort out which are right and which are not; for that is letting us off the hook, by-passing our responsibility; for God's call always increases man's active responsibility, and never diminishes us. The work of the Spirit in our hearts is healing and purifying, helping us to discern more and more clearly what is of God and what is not (cf. Heb. 5:14). So God educates us to know what to ask, and what not to ask. The saint is not the petitioner who is just more ready to accept the wisdom of God in declining our requests, but he is the man who is less likely to make the wrong petitions anyway. Here friendship with God follows a similar pattern to friendship with man: it leads to greater fellow-feeling, to greater sensitivity to the values of the other.

The problem of unanswered prayer is then the problem of sin and of lack of discernment: namely that we ask for things reflecting our selfishness rather than the love of God. But the word of intercession that comes from the Lord is efficacious, a word that does not return empty, but achieves that for which it has been sent (cf. Is. 55:10–11).

Intercessory prayer fits into the Trinitarian pattern with the rest of our prayer. For we pray in Christ who is the Word, the Logos, through whom the Father made all things, through whom the Father disposes all things, who is himself the wisdom of God (cf. 1 Cor. 1:24,30). By entering into Christ, we enter into this wisdom, into the one through whom all things are being guided and disposed; and the prayer of intercession is our sharing in that guidance and disposal. It is a sharing in Christ's role as the Logos and Mediator of the Father's will for all men.

Silence and Sound

'I tell you, if these were silent, the very stones would cry out' (Luke 19:40). 'Praise him with sounding cymbals; praise him with loud clashing cymbals' (Ps. 150:5).

The Catholic tradition in recent centuries has given a prominent place to silence in prayer practice. The rules of religious congregations and the horaria of religious houses have provided set times of silence to promote recollection and prayer: times for silent meditation and times for silence in the community. This emphasis has been linked to eucharistic piety, and the feeling that reverence for the Blessed Sacrament is more appropriately expressed by quiet devotion, a sentiment probably more operative north of the Alps. A similar esteem for silence is found in the Quaker tradition and many non-Christian religions, and is today encouraged by movements promoting bodily relaxation and mental repose.

In the Catholic tradition, the importance attached to silence has been due to the priority accorded to contemplative non-conceptual prayer; this emphasis has stressed interiority and the activity of the soul in a way that has rather devalued the role of the body, the community, symbols and words. With this soul-body dichotomy has gone a neglect of the importance of praying postures and a split between the liturgy and 'real prayer'. This compartmentalisation of man has also resulted in too intellectualist a view of the role of words in verbal prayer, and a ready assumption that articulated prayer had to mean something immediately intelligible; so in recent years there has been a depreciation of prayers such as the Rosary in which the basic point is not to keep one's mind on the words. We are now summoned to return to a more integrated view of man at prayer, seeing prayer as using and elevating all human faculties in the worship of God; and this means synthesising what has become divided, often between different traditions, namely the role of silence and of sound, the role of body, soul and mind, the place of language and that of the emptying out of thought and language.

The Importance of Sound. I start with this, because for Catholics it is the more neglected aspect, a neglect shown up by the unfamiliarity of the two quotations at the head of this chapter. In recent years, we have been faced by the role of sound in worship, first and less dramatically by the liturgical renewal, secondly and with greater force by the spread of Pentecostal forms of prayer.

It is important to see that sound and noise are traditional elements in Jewish and in Christian worship. The opposite of silence is sound rather than words; for sound is much wider than words, and introduces the role of music. The psalter regularly extols the making of a joyful noise for the Lord; we need to get the flavour of such psalm verses as: 'Make melody to our God upon the lyre' (147:7) 'clap your hands, all peoples: shout to God with loud songs of joy' (47:1) 'sing to him a new song, play skilfully on the strings, with loud shouts' (33:3) 'my soul makes its boast in the Lord; let the afflicted hear and be glad' (34:2) 'I cried aloud to him, and he was extolled with my tongue' (66:17).

As has been noted in the chapter on 'Praise and Thanksgiving', rejoicing and celebration call for audible expression in community, so that God is praised by his people. In this celebration, we are not just communicating words and concepts to each other: there is an important sense in which the medium is the message. Making a joyful noise for the Lord contains its own justification; celebration is just celebration.

So the music can be as expressive as the words, and words may be used that are really words for singing rather than saying, even words geared to shouting rather than speaking! Alleluia!

Some readers may feel that our world is full enough of noise with departing airliners and electronically boosted pop groups registering their output in decibels; and that today what we need in worship is silence. I do not deny the need for silence at all, but to urge the importance of sound in worship is not just pandering to contemporary trends; sound and silence in prayer fulfil different and complementary functions. This is another instance of our not being faced by an either-or; we are not asked to choose between being silent Christians and noisy Christians, but we are asked to be silent when the Spirit calls for silence, and to make a joyful sound when the Spirit stirs that response.

Noise achieves a letting go of ourselves. Inhibited people do not easily make a noise before others. The achieving of noise can have a break-through release effect, a loosening of the self that opens more to the action of God. Silence in a prayer-group is not automatically a sign of progress, for silence can mean different things. Silence can be empty, or it can be full; it can be the silence of death and non-activity, or it can be the expectant silence of life. We have to pray what is there within, what God gives; and it is possible to be silent, obstinately silent, when we should speak, and it is possible to make a noise when we should be silent. Sometimes people say in prayer-groups: 'Why should I inflict my prayer on others?' This wrong question ignores the will of God, and what the Spirit is doing: for the right question may be: 'Who am I to deprive the others of what the Lord is trying to give through me?'

The crisis-points, both big and small, which were mentioned in the chapter 'Growth in the Spirit', normally involve God asking us to let something go; and so we experience an inner call and pull to surrender, which much in us cries out against. It may be that we have to exult, that it is right for us to sing, but we are too shy or too proud, too afraid of what others might think, too worried about the likely unmusical outcome. It may be that we need to weep, but we fight that. In all these cases, both in learning to rejoice and in learning to grieve (the two are closely related, for you cannot learn one without eventually discovering the other), letting down the barriers to God means making some kind of noise, whether sorrowful weeping or joyful rejoicing. When we do this, yielding to God's movement within, something in us is released; we give God more space, and let him be Lord of another area of our being.

But of course not every noise is a noise for the Lord, not even every sound made in church. And not every letting go is letting God in. There is such a thing as exhibitionism; but we must not be frightened off real human expressions of joy and grief by labelling all noise-making exhibitionist.

The Value of Silence. If this is stressed less in this book, the reason is that Catholics are more familiar with the value of silence, not because of any hesitations on my part. Silence is essential, but not all the time. It plays various roles: of waiting, of maturing, of deepening, of sensitising. Silence is fundamental to a real listening to the Lord; without silence, we are unlikely to discern the subtler movements of the Spirit. We need quiet and repose, to let our minds and our imaginations wind down, to hear and to read between God's lines.

Silence often accompanies waiting, an important experience in the Christian life; waiting expresses both the faith that God will act and will guide, and the awareness that the hour has not yet come. Such waiting puts us in our rightful place, acknowledging the Lordship of Christ, that he is master of time, and that we are servants at his disposal, including time disposal. We have to learn to 'wait in joyful hope for the coming of our Saviour Jesus Christ'. Waiting is essential for our enthusiasm and all-too-human desire to be transmuted into humble and effective ministry within God's plan.

Silence also plays a vital part in deepening what God is doing in the heart, for letting the consequences of the more decisive moments develop and permeate our lives; this maturing process gets things into perspective, and guards against the danger of thinking we have got further than in fact we have. Silence is also necessary for discernment to develop: and whilst discernment may often have to operate in a context of sound, perhaps to discern what is happening in the noise, it demands a peace and a silence in the heart.

To advance in prayer, we have to be emptied out, to still our minds, to stop our thoughts racing here and there, to learn not to do anything but just to be. This aspect of silence has not been sufficiently stressed at the popular level: that not only do we need an external atmosphere of silence, but also an inner peace, a silence within. We have to be emptied of our thoughts, in order to be filled with God's; we have to clear the ground, so that God can plant his seeds.

This relationship between being emptied and being filled is important for seeing the complementarity of silence and sound, of silence and ideas. For it is only when we have become still that the Lord comes through clearly in the heart; only when we are silent within that the voice there is more readily discernible as the Lord, rather than the noisy voice of our imagination and mind. It is here that we can find the trinitarian basis for the proper relationship between silence and sound: for sounds and words that are of God arise within the silence, as the Word comes forth from the silent depths of the Father. So God's sound, his word, comes forth out of his silence, and this word then leads us back into the stillness of the Father.

It is then a mistake to accord a totally subordinate role to sound in worship, and to depreciate verbal and articulated prayer in relation to silent and non-conceptual contemplation.

The Christian is made free, free to respond to God as the Spirit leads; and a person is not yet free if he can only make a noise or if he can only be silent. Each guarantees the freedom and authenticity of the other. There is no ideal blend between silence and sound that can be established independently of seeking the Lord: the only ideal is to follow where the Spirit leads, or as it is expressed in the book of Wisdom: 'When I am silent they will wait for me, and when I speak they will give heed' (8:12).

In prayer-groups there is a particular temptation to feel that a silence has gone on too long, and something must be done: so we had better say or sing something, so here goes! To do this is to pray hollow prayers, prayers with the letter but not the Spirit; so we can repeat prayers and hymns that were right on previous occasions, because then given in the heart, and wrong now, because not so given. The ratio between silence and sound in a prayer-group will depend on the jobs the Lord has to be done, the tasks he gives, and these will often though not always be related to the needs of the participants. To say or to sing just to break the silence will prevent the real jobs from being done, which may be painful and arduous, about which we may not even know and exchanges the reality of God's battles in the world for the unreality of a mildly enjoyable but hollow repetition of a familiar pattern.

Here again the lessons to be learned from group prayer apply in fact to all forms of prayer, even praying on one's own. The relative functions of sound and silence are important in the liturgy, and it is a legitimate ground of complaint against much post-Vatican II worship that it is one continuous torrent of words. It is not an adequate defence to say that the liturgy caters for sound, and private prayer for silence. For here, as in non-liturgical prayer, there is a connection between the authenticity and depth of both silence and sound: each prepares for and builds on the other.

Within the liturgy, we need to make far more use of pauses, only beginning the prayer that follows when the moment is ripe. More use can be made of silence after the Scripture readings, with the homily perhaps coming in a more reflective mood after some silent reflection; this style of Mass is especially well suited to conferences, retreats and more intimate occasions. The same applies to the spacing of bidding prayers, in which a pause is indicated in the rubrics, though rarely observed in practice, between the petition and the 'Lord, hear us'; when the invitation is made to make spontaneous intercessions, it is important to regard periods of silence as part of the Prayer of the Faithful, and not as failure. If we know how to be silent, particularly with others, silences within the liturgy will not embarrass, nor make us look for ways of filling the void created by our lack of prayer.

Praying Postures. Just as in private prayer, Catholics have appreciated the value of silence, so with postures in prayer we have stressed the appropriateness of kneeling, and again are not alone in this emphasis. In recent times, sitting for meditation has become more popular, and is thought by the less sympathetic to be a sign of physical weakness and to show a diminution of respect for the Blessed Sacrament.

The liturgy however reminds us of a greater variety in praying postures: that times are provided for standing, for kneeling, for sitting, for prostration even, as well as various forms of movement within prayer, e.g. in processions of various degrees of solemnity and symbolic meaning.

As with silence and sound, we must see that different postures express different human dispositions and moods of prayer. No one is requiring us to choose a favourite posture: we are not asked to be kneelers or sitters, but just to pray. Within our prayer we choose the posture that is most appropriate and most expressive for our prayer on that occasion. So that just as the liturgy prescribes different postures at different times, so too in our private prayer we do well to vary our postures as appropriate.

There are two distinct purposes in regard to the position of the body in prayer. There are postures through which we pray, and postures which facilitate prayer. In the former, we express our prayer through bodily postures and gestures, as in prostration, in praying with outstretched arms, in forms of bodily movement; in the latter, we adopt bodily positions of stillness and relaxation in order to clear the mind of thought, to stop the racing of the imagination, and to focus our spiritual concentration. Both of these approaches to the role of the body are valid, reflecting the earthy and the spiritual religious traditions respectively. Again we are not faced with a choice between the two: we don't have to opt either for cruciform or yogic models, but we develop in different ways by using both.

The kneeling posture that we have come to practise tends to be neither one thing nor the other: when we kneel to pray, we are not really praying through our bodies but neither is it a posture that favours mental relaxation and bodily repose. I suspect that this has not always been so, but has resulted over the centuries from the body-soul dichotomy and the reduction of bodily gesture in kneeling, with the introduction of arm and elbow props.

Most of us need to learn how to use the body in prayer: to learn how to pray through our bodies and how to adopt postures of still repose. In each case, our prayer will become less cerebral: praying through our bodies means expressing the whole man, not just our minds, making the bodily posture part of the prayer itself, as much expression of ourselves before God as the words we say; and learning bodily repose and to be still with the Lord means switching off the mind.

Praying with the body includes gestures as well as postures. Here we may have quite extraordinary difficulty in expressing our faith through gestures, even though we may find no problem about ample gestures in a secular setting. Much of this is just the way we have been taught to pray, and the embarrassment will then disappear as the unfamiliarity wears off.

Learning to vary our postures according to the prayer we are praying will often mean beginning with one posture and ending with another. Prayer beginning in a penitential position of kneeling with bowed head or of prostration may rightly end up with raised head, the Lord saying 'Look at me, look up; stop looking at yourself; I have won the victory.' This variation of posture within prayer is not a recommendation or rationalisation of fidgeting, for restlessness is something to be overcome. No, the right changes of posture come from changes in our prayer.

There are forms of tightness of spirit that require bodily movement for release. In this, help is normally needed from a more experienced and discerning person, who may detect the tightness and need to recommend changes in posture.

The liturgy again provides a model, for every liturgy contains a variety of praying postures and gestures; and we have to learn to make these our own, and get beyond the irritation of 'having to keep bobbing up and down'. We have to rediscover for ourselves how the standing posture has always been the resurrection position, the posture for praise and thanksgiving; and to become more aware of the penitential connotations of kneeling. Most importantly, our liturgies must have more *doing* in relation to *saying*; so that the congregation has a blend of saying and doing nearer to that of the celebrant. This must be a primary source of Christian people learning to pray through sacramental actions.

Prayer groups can be helpful for learning to pray with others in various postures without embarrassment. We know then that we can truly pray when we are sitting, upright or cross-legged, and this removes the fear in private prayer that we are not really praying when we are neither kneeling nor thinking!

In this matter of silence, sound, postures and gestures, we should expect considerable variation according to age. It is natural that there should be more vigorous sound and more ample gestures among the young; and this is not merely a matter of available energy. It also reflects the process of spiritual growth. For it is natural that the stages of spiritual development requiring deep lettings go, and crisis experiences should come in our earlier years of Christian life; and that the closing stages of our lives should be marked by a greater serenity and less drama. This is the way it should be: for it is far easier for younger people to change, to open up areas that are closed; but as we know not all people grow spiritually in their adolescence and mature adulthood, and some come to old age with wounds deeper and more established than in their youth and with little natural flexibility of spirit. Here we must trust in God, with whom all things are possible, and let the Lord do it his way, yet respecting the age and limitations of those in such need.

The Discernment of Spirits

All movements of the Spirit in Christian history demonstrate the need for discernment of spirits and for wisdom, both mentioned by St. Paul as charismata of the New Covenant (cf. 1 Cor. 12:8, 10). When no need is felt for these two activities of the Spirit, it is a bad sign; for the devil has little incentive to produce the counterfeit and seduce the elect when a state of apathy and torpor prevails, such as that condemned in such strong terms in Rev. 3:15-16. When things are really happening for the Lord, the forces of evil will counter-attack; this sequence has been constantly verified in the lives of the saints. It is worth noting the key place occupied by discernment of spirits in the Spiritual Exercises of St. Ignatius; for these exercises were designed as a powerful weapon for winning souls whole-heartedly for Jesus Christ.

What is discernment? Discernment is the activity of detecting the source and the thrust of particular phenomena and manifestations: whence they come and where they lead. 'Beloved, do not believe every spirit, but test the spirits to see whether they are of God; for many false prophets have gone out into the world' (1 John 4:1). It is therefore to be distinguished from understanding and knowledge, a point that is evident from St. Paul's listing a word of wisdom and a word of knowledge separate from the ability to distinguish spirits. A certain priority, at least a temporal priority, should be given to discernment over understanding; for whilst we may want to know the reasons for particular forms of behaviour, it is more immediately important from a Christian point of view to know whether something is from the Holy Spirit, or from some other quarter. Understanding to some degree will regularly follow, but this is often less urgent than detecting the basic drift and direction of behaviour, of events and of lives. God will indicate what we need to know when we need to know, and this will often be far from a total understanding of the situation, particularly at the moment when basic discernment is crucial.

Discernment is then not only the work of detecting the presence and operations of the evil one; it includes sensing what God is doing in a particular situation, which way he is beckoning and what in particular phenomena is of the spirit of man alone, being neither the work of the Spirit of God nor that of evil spirits.

Who can discern? We must here affirm the basic competence of every Christian to discern, the competence that flows from the presence of the Spirit of God. This ability to discern is directly proportionate to personal holiness; for the Christian filled with the Spirit of God naturally detects what is of God and what is not. 'No one comprehends the thoughts of God except the Spirit of God' (1 Cor. 2:11). This connaturality has its natural basis in that any person who really loves can detect the presence of hatred and resentment. This discernment is not so much miraculous illumination as the Spirit purifying and elevating a natural process.

But we must also affirm that there is a charisma, a gift of discernment of spirits, that mentioned in 1 Cor. 12:10, which like the other gifts of the Spirit goes beyond the recipient's degree of sanctification and is given for the sake of the whole Christian community. As with other particular vocations, such as those of priest and prophet, the existence of the distinct charism, given to some but not to all, interacts with and presupposes the like gift given to all the baptised. The particular charism is a reminder of the endowment of every Christian and serves to dissuade us from drawing conclusions from the exercise of spiritual gifts to the possession of personal holiness.

Like all the charismata, discernment must be exercised in conjunction with the gifts given to others within the community. So we should not expect any one person to discern everything, even one with a reputation for holiness. For God may reveal part of what is happening to one person and part to another; and the whole picture may only be pieced together by Christian sharing. So if in a community, we are concerned about the life and prayer of one member, we should share our concern in prayer with our brothers; the resulting prayer will be the care of the community for a sick member, not the private activities of a self-appointed private eye.

When to discern? There is a common misunderstanding that discernment is only necessary when things are going wrong. This is mistaken, for discernment must be part of the way we live. We need discernment at all times to discern what we should be doing and what we should be praying at that time. It is like the human sense of smell, which is always there ready to pick up an offending odour or a sweet scent. According to what we pick up, we respond, by intercession, by thanksgiving, in whatever way is given.

When discernment is not part of our daily life, we fail to spot until far too late when things have gone wrong, and got out of focus. We then become fearful, prone to blanket condemnations and repressive measures, that represent a failure to discern precisely what is wrong and where.

How to discern? We can consider both the prerequisites and the criteria for discernment. The necessary prerequisites are deep lives of union with Jesus Christ, together with an awareness of the need and confident faith that the Lord will meet this need. Discernment comes from the Lord, and must be sought from the Lord. For this reason it is inseparable from prayer: both as the proper context in which discernment is sought and as that within which it is given.

The criteria for discernment are numerous, and it may be helpful to look briefly at some of those given in the New Testament.

Fruits: 'You will know them by their fruits. Are grapes gathered from thorns, or figs from thistles? So, every sound tree bears good fruit, but the bad tree bears evil fruit' (Matt. 7:16–17). St. Paul provides us with a list of the fruit (singular) of the Holy Spirit in Galatians: 'love, joy, peace, patience, kindness, goodness, faithfulness, gentleness, self-control' (5:22–23). Of these, love, joy, peace and self-control can usefully be selected for further examination (patience and faithfulness having in fact featured in other contexts in previous chapters).

Love is presented in several New Testament passages as the sign that God is at work among Christians. 'We know that we have passed out of death into life, because we love the brethren' (1 John 3:14), a sign then for ourselves. 'By this all men will know that you are my disciples, if you have love for one another' (John 13:35), a sign for all men, for the world. This is another way of stating St. Paul's teaching about the gifts of the Spirit being for the benefit of all, and the upbuilding of the Church in love: 'since you are eager for manifestations of the Spirit, strive to excel in building up the Church' (1 Cor. 14:12). See too 1 Cor. 12:7 and Eph. 4:11–12.

In the New Testament love is not seen as merely subjective, as how I am feeling, but as a visible reality, expressed in bonds joining people to one another. It is essentially visible, and so provides an appropriate measure for discerning whether an apparently charismatic figure is really animated by the Spirit of God. The key question then is: 'Is his life and work truly upbuilding the Body of Christ in love?' This is not the same question as 'Is he rocking the boat?', but is asking whether any rocking is leading to deeper faith and love.

Joy is a keynote of St. Paul's epistle to the Philippians, but is a common enough theme in the entire Pauline corpus. 'For the kingdom of God is not food and drink, but righteousness and peace and joy in the Holy Spirit' (Rom. 14:17). 'May the God of hope fill you with all joy and peace in believing' (Rom. 15:13).

We are probably more suspicious of joy as a criterion than of the other fruits in the Pauline list; partly because it appears the most subjective, partly because we confuse it with joviality and being jolly. In fact, the joy of the Spirit like all the fruits is very different from all artificially induced human moods: for the Spirit frees, the Spirit increases sensitivity, the Spirit evokes wonder and gratitude for all God's creation, leading to prayer and praise. The joy of the Spirit is a rejoicing in God; St. Paul says: 'I rejoice in the Lord greatly' about the Philippians' renewed concern for himself (Phil. 4:10). Its spirit is expressed above all in the Magnificat of Our Lady, whose spirit 'rejoices in God my Saviour' (Luke 1:47). If we think this criterion too subjective, it may be because we mistake it for something less than the true fruit of the Spirit!

Where joy does have its limitations as a criterion is in regard to its permanence. For whilst love is or always should be present, there are times when the most saintly Christian would hardly describe himself as rejoicing: though God's Spirit opens the possibility of rejoicing even in suffering for the name of Jesus (cf. Col. 1:24). The questions here then more aptly concern whether we ever rejoice and the characteristics of that rejoicing, whether they bear the marks of the Spirit or of intoxication 'of the flesh'.

Peace is brought by Jesus Christ: 'Peace I leave with you; my peace I give to you; not as the world gives do I give to you' (John 14:27). Peace is the blessing contained in the Jewish greeting *Shalom*, and Jesus brings that peace a deeper meaning and content which is *his* peace. This is contrasted with the peace known by the world, the peace of appeasement, the peace of compromise, of cold wars, of live and let live.

'And let the peace of Christ rule in your hearts, to which indeed you were called in the one body' (Col. 3:15). The Spirit brings peace in the heart, a stilling of violence and unrest within: Jesus tells us 'What comes out of the mouth proceeds from the heart, and this defiles a man' (Matt. 15:18), and this is reversed by the Spirit's healing work within; from the mouth of the Christian come words of peace, so that he is a peacemaker, of whom Jesus says 'Blessed are the peacemakers, for they shall be called sons of God' (Matt. 5:9). A test of peace in the heart is in our words; are we men of peaceful words?

Self-control is mentioned here because it may appear to contrast with the section on 'letting go', on letting down our barriers. For it is self-control to which we readily appeal as a reason for not making any leap. In fact, real Christian control of self is something other than battening down the hatches, maintenance of a stiff upper lip, and not letting the side down before others. The self-control of the Spirit means greater freedom of self-disposition, being set free within; it is being more fully under our own control because we are more controlled by the Spirit of God.

Letting go may lead to apparent disorder (remember Christian 'letting go' has already been distinguished from all forms of self-centred exhibitionism), and some of the visible consequences may appear not to be fruits of the Spirit. But spiritual release involves something being released; and what are released are the things that need healing. In such cases the real work of the Spirit of God will lead into greater peace, and the growth in true self-control will follow later. Peace is thus a more immediate test of the rightness of 'lettings go', not in the sense that the acts of release will be peaceful, but that they lead into peace. The work of the evil one always tends in the opposite direction away from deep inner peace, either to visible agitation or to lifeless apathy masquerading as peace.

This has brought us to the central Pauline idea of *freedom*, to which Christ calls us (Gal. 5:13) and for which 'Christ has set us free' (Gal. 5:1). This freeing work of the Spirit restores in us the true image of God, so that we become authentically ourselves, the persons God has made us to be. We are freed from the worship of idols, from the tyranny of convention, from all that makes us put on different masks in difficult situations, from all aping and the need to seek approval, from the thraldom of lies and half-truths.

An important criterion for discernment is whether greater freedom is resulting. This is not just a matter of whether conventions are being overthrown, but of what is replacing them. Some milieux vigorously asserting their own degree of emancipation have merely exchanged one form of slavery for another: the tyranny of conformist conventions for the tyranny of nonconformist conventions.

But the Spirit of God does not merely change patterns of behaviour, but liberates from within: it leads to greater creativity, to greater variety and so to greater unpredictability. The Spirit does not standardise, does not provide detailed recipes, does not computerise and manipulate. The more growth is from God, the greater variety there will be, and the richness will be that of the mature Body of Christ. No saint is a replica of another saint; no community of holy people is identical with any other community of holy people.

Real freedom and variety result from seeking the face of the Lord, not from attempts to copy apparently successful lives and models. 'The Lord looks down from heaven upon the children of men, to see if there are any that act wisely, that seek after God' (Ps. 14:2).

The freedom and variety test is particularly important in evaluating the results of enthusiastic religion of whatever form. But whilst an absence of seeking, a lack of any interest or zeal, is a bad sign, the degree of openness to the Spirit cannot be measured by enthusiasm alone. For enthusiasts all suffer the temptation to create others in their own image and likeness, rather than allowing the Lord to fashion them in his. This can result in a growing lack of freedom in what seem at first appearance highly informal and spontaneous forms of worship. For printed rubrics, which rightly understood free us for prayer, are replaced by unprinted rubrics, which tell us how to pray; and so apparent spontaneity can become highly stereotyped. So with prayer-groups we need to ask: are our times of prayer always the same? do we try to make fresh meetings like previous ones? are any new stages in personal, group and community life noticeable? Answers indicating a lack of variety are counter-signs to give us pause, and to suggest an examination of aims and priorities.

This brings us to a fundamental test in the discernment of spirits, that we can call *focus*: this is what we are seeking, the direction we are facing, the focal point of our life and prayer endeavours. This is a test equally applicable to ourselves as to other people: what are we seeking? what are they seeking?

However, our own seeking of the Lord is never total, and there is always something mixed, parts of us that are not yet given to the Lord, either being held back or of which we are not yet conscious, and parts that are truly seeking him. From whatever uncertainty or confusion we begin our adult lives, a fundamental direction in the heart and will is likely to emerge. We cannot spend a lifetime sitting on the fence, the truth expressed by Jesus in his words: 'No one can serve two masters; for either he will hate the one and love the other, or he will be devoted to the one and despise the other. You cannot serve God and mammon' (Matt. 6:24).

But for those fundamentally facing God, there are parts that remain unintegrated and need healing; and for those serving mammon, there are pockets of something higher, once-held hopes and desires not totally extinguished, remnants of the idealism of youth perhaps, dreams not entirely banished from consciousness. But these pockets and remnants, whether of God or of mammon, are not where our hearts are now; they are not the way we are now facing, but they are possible causes of future changes of direction, either way.

The focus of prayer and life is a fundamental criterion which can be applied on the instant; by contrast, the test of the fruits requires time, for the fruits must always be compared with what went before, what has replaced what, a comparison that provides a more reliable guide after a space of time. The focal point can often be sensed by a discerning and spiritually sensitive Christian without previous acquaintance, and is a criterion of readiest access during times of prayer. So that within prayer we must ourselves want to pray, and to seek the Lord, and the more we do this, the quicker we shall pick up when others are seeking something other than God. A simple but not trivial example concerns outbursts of laughter in prayer-groups: if something amusing happens quite unintentionally, it is natural to laugh and to keep on praying. But there is often a temptation to cap something funny, to prolong the laughter, and when this occurs the focus has slipped from praying to being funny. The same applies when people make much of laughter to show how free and uninhibited they are: 'I thank you, God, that our group is free, uninhibited, and able to laugh . . .' has a ring not unlike the prayer of the Pharisee in Luke 18:10–14..

Within any prayer-situation, the important thing is to keep praying: this is vital for the prayer-group to be true to what it has assembled to do, and vital for discernment to be possible. If any unexpected things happen—an emotional outburst, or someone praying most unusual prayers—the immediate discernment test is that of focus: what is this person's focus? what is he seeking? If he is truly praying and seeking the Lord, even though in a way that causes us embarrassment or irritation, then the embarrassment or the irritation is the price of charity; people can only pray as they are, and if they are odd, immature, agitated, depressed, then that is how they are and where they have to start praying. So we cannot discern solely on the basis of present state of disturbance or abnormality: for them that may represent progress. We can test focus and direction now; and we can compare present disturbance with past disturbance, which is applying the criteria of the fruits of the Spirit.

The mention of disturbance is not to suggest that prayer-groups do or should abound in dramatic outbursts and alarming occurrences; rather it is at these times that we are most tempted to substitute other criteria, e.g. of respectability, of reputation, of safety-first, for those of discernment.

The level of thanksgiving in people's prayer, mentioned as an important test of the rightness of prayer in the chapter on 'Praise and Thanksgiving', is in fact part of the focus and direction. Those who spontaneously thank God for everything have their focus right: they see God as the giver of all good things. Whereas those who do not thank are unlikely to have that focus on the Lord.

The *Incarnation* is another criterion given prominence in the New Testament. St. John writes: 'By this you know the Spirit of God: every spirit which confesses that Jesus Christ has come in the flesh is of God, and every spirit which does not confess Jesus is not of God' (1 John 4:2-3).

Man has a constant tendency towards a more purely spiritual religion than the incarnate faith of the Christian Church. So we may be attracted to a form of religion that excludes the glorification of the flesh, the gory details of Calvary, the earthiness of human gestures, the fire of human passions, and instead to seek a pure angelic aethereal worship, alleged to be 'in spirit and in truth'. But the Holy Spirit is the Spirit of Jesus, the Spirit through whom the Word became flesh; and the work of God's Spirit always enfleshes, and glorifies that flesh. The fruits of the Spirit, love, joy, peace, patience, kindness, goodness, faithfulness, gentleness, self-control, are all embodied incarnate fruits. There is no guarantee whatever of the presence of the Holy Spirit on the grounds of extraordinary powers and phenomena: as Our Lord foretold of the end times: 'For false Christs and false prophets will arise and show great signs and wonders, so as to lead astray, if possible, even the elect' (Matt. 24:24). But the wonders and works of the false prophets will not produce the fruits of the Spirit of God, they will not upbuild the incarnate Body of Christ, though they may appear very 'spiritual' to the undiscerning.

The possibility of the counterfeit should not lead Christians to deny or ignore that great things are done by God through and in witness to Jesus Christ. The Gospel is confirmed by the signs that attend it (cf. Mark 16:20) and through such signs the Holy Spirit acts as witness (cf. Acts 5:32). Apart from the more obvious danger of rationalising our mediocrity, there can be an inverted pride in the attitude that our generation and modern scientific man does not need or cannot believe in the wonders that are the signs of God. Signs call for discernment; no signs call for a different form of concern.

Ministry and Discernment. Whilst the discernment of spirits is not a responsibility and charism restricted to the clergy, it has a special importance for the Christian priest or minister and is an explicit responsibility of those in positions of pastoral oversight. We can then distinguish the element of discernment within all ministry as such, and the discernment that is *episcopē*, the discernment of those responsible for the government and guidance of the Church.

Within all ministering, there is an element of discernment, because the minister has to discern what God is wanting to give through his ministry. Visiting a sick patient, what does the priest say? It is only if we pray, and within our praying seek what the Lord is doing and indicating, that we will really speak God's Word to that person in that situation: if we do not pray and seek what the Lord is giving, we are likely to be giving our pet advice, our standard recipe, our stock answers. This need to pray and discern is all the more obvious in cases when we just do not know the situation: and we must be open to the possibility that the Lord just wants us to love, rather to know all that is wrong, and even that he will give the healing Word to someone else. For we must always remember that Christ has many members, and that the most important and the most exciting work is sometimes given to others!

For those in positions of pastoral oversight, there is the difficulty of distance from that which is being discerned; in this, it would seem that the criteria for discernment requiring time for mature judgment, e.g. the fruits of the Spirit and the test of the Incarnation, are the most appropriate, combined with consultation with those more directly involved at the grass roots, who will need to concentrate more on the criterion of focus or direction. 'Do not quench the Spirit, do not despise prophesying, but test everything; hold fast what is good, abstain from every form of evil' (1 Thess. 5:19-22).

God The Giver of Tasks

A glaring gap exists in the Christian world between spirituality and social commitment; to the non-Christian it must seem as though Christians are forced to choose between the two, so that either we stake all on prayer and spirituality, or we embrace the social gospel and commit ourselves to political reform. In today's terminology, it is the gap between charismatic renewal and political theology.

Throughout this book, the attempt has been made within the consideration of prayer and worship to bridge the gap between the personal and the social, and to integrate liturgical and communal worship into our understanding of all prayer. Social responsibility is treated only indirectly, just as personal responsibility has only been so treated. I have no more treated of the political than I have of the domestic; but both equally should be related to prayer, for God is the creator and sustainer of the social as of the personal.

A key idea for the reconciliation of the personal and the social is that God has a particular will for each group and for each social structure as he has for each person; God is in every place promoting, urging, prodding man to love and to liberate not just through the minds and hearts of individuals, but through the activities and processes of social groupings and the structures of society. The great biblical images taken up throughout the liturgy—the images of the city, of the Kingdom, of the banquet—are social, and if they are not related to our social experience, their liturgical use is but sentimental fantasy.

A false assumption often lurking beneath the person-society antithesis is that the prayer-person, the pietist, believes that God acts personally in the lives of individuals and at best ignores whether he does the same in social groupings, whereas the society-person, the reformer, sees God as a liberating force within society, having a general will for justice and freedom, yet indifferent to the details.

The need to seek God's Will applies equally to both the personal and the social dimensions of life; and in fact it is impossible to live fully by faith without believing in and seeking God's particular will in every human situation.

Faith in the particular will of God means that God gives us our tasks at all levels of human life; both to individuals and to communities. So God gives me this job, and a different task is given to someone else; this work is given to this group, a different work to that. This is not like the allocation of duties by a military commander, for the relationship between God and man is not that of a human authority and its subordinates; God's Will does not lessen man's choice, but creates and develops it.

Prayer is indispensable for discovering the tasks that God is giving. Well-intentioned people readily start their charitable careers by supporting a plethora of good causes, and great dispersion of energy can result. We know from experience how easily enthusiastic supporters of good causes can expend a vast amount of effort exhausting themselves in good works, and yet somehow looking back how little was really achieved! We may comfort ourselves with the thought that we cannot measure how much good we did, and that only God knows the final score. There is truth in this, but we do know from the lives of holy people that quite extraordinary results can be achieved by complete openness to the Will of God. The lives of men like St. Vincent de Paul and St. John Bosco, and in our day of a woman like Mother Teresa of Calcutta, show how complete openness to God's loving care produces prodigious achievements, quite disproportionate to the amount of human effort and planning.

Our work will only be productive for God when we realise that he is already at work, and that the Kingdom of God is built up by the coalescence of the work of God and the work of man. So many of our activities, even the best and most important, are too much the work of men implementing their remedy with good will, without really seeking what God is doing, and where he is leading. Recent writing of a more secularising kind has been right to emphasise that when Christians enter a particular milieu—a factory, an office or a government department—they do not take God to where he was not present before; but it has been wrong in the implication that God's Will only extends to a general desire for justice, truth and freedom.

But at this point an obvious problem arises as far as groups and societies are concerned; for the social groupings in our world are pluralist in religion, and are made up of believers in various faiths, Christian and non-Christian, and of non-believers of varying degrees of militancy or tolerance. Is it not practically impossible to seek God's Will in such a society? Can more be done than a general promotion of the majority view of the common good?

Here there are enormous difficulties; but this is the size of the task of evangelisation. What we Christians are called to do is to live to the utmost our own faith; which means that Christians with common concerns and responsibilities must learn to relate these together to God, the giver, in thanksgiving, in contrition and in intercession as we should personally for our personal tasks and responsibilities. When we say that the Church is the sacrament of God's saving work, we mean that the Christian community should live as God wills all society to live.

Our task here has not been facilitated by over-simplified views of Christian involvement in society: as though the choice for each Christian is simply between withdrawing into a Christian ghetto or going out as leaven in the world. But it is not just single Christians who are called to be a leaven, but also Christian groups; and with both individuals and communities there are rhythms and different patterns in the Lord's sending out and calling in. We have to ignore general dicta about involvement and retreat, and discover the pattern the Lord is giving to us and to our communities.

Our Christian weakness in relating prayer to corporate concerns is not just due to our pluralist situation, but is also brought about by our failure in wholly Christian communities to pray together and so to seek the Lord's Will in all basic decisions. Here we have a right to expect houses of religious and of clergy to set an example: to pray together, referring to the Lord in confident faith their common concerns—asking together for communal guidance, seeking together their communal vocation, thanking the Lord together for the blessings given to the group.

We can now look at some of the practical implications for both individuals and for groups in seeking the Will of God for them in every human situation; the examples whether individual or communal are applicable one to the other.

First, all human responsibility is exercised within the activity of God, and more specifically within the active Lordship of Jesus Christ; God 'has put all things under his feet and has made him the head over all things' (Eph. 1:22). So all man's workings are grounded in God, and so our role is relativised. Faith in God, the giver of tasks, recognises that he gives a work to each man, and so there are tasks he does not give to me or to my group. These may be tasks which I covet, which I think I could do far better than others, for which I am particularly well equipped; but the man of faith (and the community of faith) can let such things be done by others. Our dispensability is our strength; the true Christian is open to receiving the tasks God is giving for so long as he is giving them, and he is ready to relinquish them and move on, when that is indicated.

Secondly, the man who receives his work from God in faith must live it by faith. This is the secret of those prodigious achievements of the saints: it is not only that the faithful man believes that God is calling him to this work, but also that its daily fulfilment is equally given by the Lord. Depth of achievement comes with living this truth right down to the smallest details of life; for to be a man of faith is to live by *every* word that proceeds from the mouth of God. This is not achieved in an instant but it is our Christian ideal. We do not merely seek justice in general, but justice in this situation as it comes from the hand of God. A failure to live this out is surely at the root of the scandal at Corinth denounced by St. Paul: 'When one of you has a grievance against a brother, does he dare go to law before the unrighteous instead of the saints?' (1 Cor. 6:1). The scandal is not so much that of exposing our dirty linen in public, but that the obstinacy that leads to court is a counter-witness to living by faith; Christians at odds with each other ought to be able to come together to place their differences before the Lord in humble prayer, for as Christians both parties believe in a loving Father who guides his children by the light of his Spirit. Such prayer together does not necessarily produce a quasi-revealed solution; but to pray sincerely, we have to abdicate our own self-righteousness, to admit the possibility that we may not be wholly in the right. The very conditions of real prayer begin to break the deadlock.

Thirdly, the God who allocates the tasks gives the capacity and the power to fulfil them. St. Paul's teachings on the gifts of the Holy Spirit, the charismata, in Rom. 12:4–8 and 1 Cor. 12 are in the context of the upbuilding of the whole body and emphasise the complementarity of God's gifts. The gifts given to individuals are for the sake of the whole body (cf. 1 Cor. 12:7) and at the end of St. Paul's instances (not an exhaustive list as no two New Testament lists are anything like the same! God's giving is greater even than St. Paul's instancing) he writes 'All these are inspired by one and the same Spirit, who apportions to each one individually as he wills' (1 Cor. 12:11). Vocation and empowering go together.

Fourthly, seeking the will of God in each situation is indispensable for the inner purification of our thoughts and desires. To seek justice in society without seeking the particular will of God in prayer is to try to establish the Kingdom of God by merely human means. The person who throws himself into any and every good cause and who has not yet learned that he is not called to do everything by himself is still too self-willed, and has the universe too centred on himself; to acknowledge Jesus Christ as Lord, that he is in charge of everything and not ourselves, is the start of a long purifying and cleansing process, whereby we are purged and refined of our self-will, our desire to dominate and our need to be in on everything. 'For no other foundation can any one lay than that which is laid, which is Jesus Christ. Now if any one builds on the foundation with gold, silver, precious stones, wood, hay, straw—each man's work will become manifest; for the Day will disclose it, because it will be revealed with fire, and the fire will test what sort of work each one has done' (1 Cor. 3:11–13). It is only as we are cleansed and re-made in the likeness of Jesus Christ that God can do through us the wonders he did through Jesus; this surely is part of the meaning of those words in St. John: 'Truly, truly, I say to you, he who believes in me will also do the works that I do; and greater works than these will he do, because I go to the Father' (14:12). The unproductiveness of so much of our energetic commitment is caused by its mixed character; we think we are just doing the works of God, but in fact we are partly still doing our own thing, meeting our own needs, and setting ourselves up as lords.

This combination of great effort and small achievement is

often a sign of human obstinacy; we are determined to work for God, to build up this apostolate, to reform this structure, but in our way, with our resources, according to our theories. But perhaps we do not allow ourselves to work *with* God, rather than *for* God. Trying too hard is a spiritual malaise, experienced both in the active Church-worker, clerical and lay, and in regard to prayer. When our efforts don't seem to lead anywhere, the remedy is prayer to put all in God's hands; merely redoubling our effort makes things twice as bad! We are given this lesson in the story in John 21, when Simon Peter says 'I am going fishing' and the others with him say 'We will go with you' (21:3). And we are told: 'They went out and got into the boat; but that night they caught nothing' (21:3). But next morning Jesus tells them: 'Cast the net on the right side of the boat, and you will find some.' So they cast it, and now they were not able to haul it in, for the quantity of fish' (21:6).

No doubt labouring all night for no return is sometimes a valuable experience for teaching us that 'Unless the Lord builds the house, those who build it labour in vain' (Ps. 127:1). But as we grow in spiritual sensitivity, we should get the feel more quickly as to whether our efforts are leading anywhere, whether the Lord is Lord of our work, or whether we are labouring in vain. For labour in vain is normally not accompanied by prayer; and the more regular and continuous our prayer becomes, the less long should we spend in fruitless labours of our own devising.

For most of us the energy of youth and of the prime of life is often spent in this way, and it may be only with the diminution of physical strength in later years and a recognition of our limitations that we hand it over to the Lord's guidance. 'Truly, truly, I say to you, when you were young, you girded yourself and walked where you would; but when you are old, you will stretch out your hands, and another will gird you and carry you where you do not wish to go' (John 21:18).

These words to St. Peter have echoes in Cardinal Newman's hymn *Lead, kindly Light*: 'I loved to choose and see my path; but now lead Thou me on', words that sprang from the exhaustion of near-fatal sickness.

Finally, acknowledging the Lordship of Jesus Christ over all human affairs and the particular will of God for every detail of life means accepting that it is God who prepares us for the tasks he is giving. Looking back in our lives, it is astonishing how the eye of faith can see how God was preparing us for later tasks, without at the time our having any inkling of the future, perhaps even with our regarding that time as wasted and unproductive.

Recognising the preparatory work of God involves accepting that there are tasks for which we are being prepared, but for which we are not yet ready. 'My hour has not yet come' (John 2:4). This is not an endorsement of older methods of priestly training which postponed all forms of pastoral involvement until the candidate was fully formed; none the less we must be open to the possibility of saying 'No' to jobs because we are not yet ready. We take our situations to the Lord in prayer, and if we are not ready he will show us; so that then to take on the task would be a running away from rather than a running with the Lord.

When considering the tasks God gives in the world, we must point to the reconciling aspect of the mission of Jesus Christ. 'For he is our peace, who has made us both one, and has broken down the dividing wall of hostility' (Eph. 2:14); these words, originally written of the fallen barrier between Jews and Gentiles, apply to all divisions between people—barriers of race, of religion, of ideology, of social class, of sex, of traditional vendetta. 'There is neither Jew nor Greek, there is neither slave nor free; there is neither male nor female; for you are all one in Christ Jesus' (Gal. 3:28).

Whether our social involvement includes a reconciling dimension is an important test of its Christian spirit; for the tasks given by God are ultimately reconciling tasks. That does not mean that they are obviously conciliatory; they may be deeply disturbing and initially divisive, as were many of the prophetic actions recorded in the Scriptures. But Jesus does not set out to divide men; men are divided by the preaching of the Gospel, not because the Lord wants division, but because of the hardness of heart that refuses to hear.

But this division between the meek and the hard of heart never follows our social lines of race, religion, class or party. The Christian who truly reconciles is no pacifier in the weak sense, but is that awkward person who fits into none of our ready-made categories, to whom no label can easily be applied. He is so fully committed that all our party-commitments are too narrow. Such a reconciler will experience the truth taught by St. Paul that it is the Cross of Jesus that has broken all barriers (cf. Eph. 2:14–16; Col. 1:21–22; 2:14); for he will suffer misunderstanding, not only from the hardhearted, but from those with whose ideals he identifies himself but whose labels he refuses.

We are brought back to the Gospel criteria for success and to the deep mystery of the life, death and resurrection of Jesus Christ, to whom God entrusted his task, and in whom we are given our tasks.

God the Breaker of Idols

An underlying theme in this book is that spiritual growth into Christ is a process of abandoning our idols, and coming to serve ever more fully the real, living God. The final words of St. John's first epistle 'Little children, keep yourselves from idols' (1 John 5:21) are not the irrelevant mutterings of a dear old man, but the perceptive advice of a wise and experienced man of God.

The story of the Israelites turning from their God to worship a golden calf is a cautionary tale of lasting importance. For as the Israelites knew, it is much pleasanter to have the security of slavery, of knowing where the next meal is coming from, of having a steady routine and fixed habits, than to bear the insecurity of being on the march with Yahweh.

The life of faith looks like radical insecurity, but is in fact making the most High our refuge, and saying to the Lord 'My refuge and my fortress', as depicted in Ps. 91 and in the exploits of the heroes of faith given in Heb. 11. 'By faith Abraham obeyed when he was called to go out to a place which he was to receive as an inheritance; and he went out not knowing where he was to go' (11:8). To live by faith is to live in trust and hope: 'For he looked forward to the city which has foundations, whose builder and maker is God' (11:10).

By contrast, the life of idolatry has an alluring security with its hope in the visibly powerful, in the immediately tangible, or in the words of the Old Testament, in the prince and in the horse. But in fact all forms of idolatry are an elevation of the gifts of God to be more than they really are; the process begins whenever we exaggerate some gift, and expect more from it than it is meant to give, and we begin to worship it. We can idolise human beings, forget their limitations, and expect more from them than they can give; we want other people to tell us what to do, saving us the labour and faith of decision; we are infatuated with calf-love; we elaborate routines which replace the seeking of God's Will, and fabricate techniques for prayer, for spreading the Church, for winning converts.

We have to admit that part of us wants to be enslaved; this is our spiritual dilemma. This is true even of those who boast loudly of their freedom and their emancipation from the bonds of the past. For whilst every form of rigid traditionalism is a form of idolatry, turning past patterns for all their goodness and one-time suitability into an absolute, so too is every pursuit of the latest fashion; there is no one less free than the person who has to be 'with it'. Whenever we expect more from a new line of thought, from a new movement in the Church, from a new regime in Church or nation, than it is able to give, we are on the path of idolatry. So we can idolise Vatican II, the liturgical renewal, theologians, democratic processes, etc., all good in themselves, but we expect more from them than they can give; we overlook their gift-character, and we separate the gifts from the Giver, who alone makes them what they truly are, who plants them and who gives their increase.

All Christians face this dilemma in regard to their own Church tradition: namely, the temptation to separate the tradition from the Spirit that gives it life, and to trust in the tradition rather than in its animator. We can be tempted to seek from Church authorities, from spiritual guides, even from rebel gurus, approval that short-circuits faith and trust in the Lord. This is where the age-old problem of the Law and the Gospel hits us. No man on earth can be our substitute in the decisions of faith: we cannot get another to trust for us. On the other hand, none of us can stand alone without our brothers and sisters in faith; we need the Church community which proclaims the Word of God, which transmits the wisdom of the ages, which safeguards the height and the depth, the length and the breadth, of the mystery of Christ. This is the context in which alone we can grow in faith, within which we learn to discern the Lord's handiwork and the wiles of the enemy. It is a community of faith. But with these inestimable gifts that the Lord has given his Church, there is the same danger as with all his gifts to man, that man can substitute the gifts for the Giver. The Church has to guard against living by mutual back-slapping and by self-sufficiency instead of living by faith in the all-giving Father.

We find this tendency to idolatry illustrated at many points in Scripture. We find man falling down before the inspiring message-bearer: 'And he said to me "These are true words of God." Then I fell down at his feet to worship him, but he said to me, "You must not do that! I am a fellow servant with you and your brethren who hold the testimony of Jesus. Worship God"' (Rev. 19:9-10).

The permanent relevance of this lesson is shown by the recurring anxiety of people to seek spiritual gurus who will solve their every problem. Anyone giving talks on prayer will know what this means: the anxiety of people worried as to whether they are on the right track, worried souls who have received conflicting advice from different sources, people concerned lest they are missing out on something. In all these cases, there is a failure to trust God. If we are worried about whether we are on the right track, no human authority can still the anxiety for long; if we ask many men for advice, it will never be unanimous; when we fear lest we miss out, it is never God whom we are afraid to miss out on! Living by faith means entrusting ourselves to God's guidance, saying: 'You are my rock, and my fortress and my deliverer' (Ps. 18:2). That we should seek advice is right, both because of our personal bias and weakness, and because God gives wisdom through others; but the right asking for advice is never idolatry. It is in prayer that we ask God to lead us to the right adviser; and that when we do ask, we do so simply and in trust.

What advice should we expect? What advice did Jesus give? 'All this Jesus said to the crowds in parables; indeed he said nothing to them without a parable' (Matt. 13:34). When people bring troubles to Jesus, he never just tells them what to do: the questions put to him are constantly answered by parables, by riddles, by questions put in return. 'One of the multitude said to him, "Teacher, bid my brother divide the inheritance with me." But he said to him, "Man, who made me a judge or divider over you?"' (Luke 12:13-14). We can think too of the story of Martha and Mary (Luke 10:38-42) and that of the rich young man (Mark 10:17-22). What is common to these episodes is the invitation to faith, that Jesus never seeks to enslave people to himself. This explains his words to the rich young man 'Why do you call me good? No one is good but God alone' (Mark 10:18). The true Christian minister always points away from himself to God; he can only help others if he is himself seeking guidance from the Lord. Then only does he minister rather than dominate.

Thanksgiving and simplicity are essential safeguards against idolatry. Thanksgiving is fundamental, because idolatry is worshipping the gift instead of the Giver. Giving thanks to God acknowledges the gift-character of the good things we are tempted to over-value. Giving thanks develops an attitude of sensitivity to all God's giving, strengthening faith, the very opposite of idolatry. Simplicity and the ability to admit mistakes, to be able to laugh at oneself, are vital too; for all exaggeration of the importance of created things involves a false solemnity, a building up of atmosphere, a development of propaganda, and a loss of humour. Movements and organisations in the Church, which may have a point, but which become self-important and pompous, lose all sense of perspective, and act as though their progress or decline is identical with the success or failure of the Church. An important role of true faith is to prick these bubbles, to laugh at all forms of pretension, and to restore our sense of the ridiculous! And all forms of idolatry are fundamentally ridiculous, a point grasped by the authors of Ps. 115 and Isa. 44:9–20: 'Our God is in the heavens; he does whatever he pleases. Their idols are silver and gold, the work of men's hands. They have mouths, but do not speak; they have eyes, but do not see; ears, but do not hear; noses, but do not smell. They have hands, but do not feel; feet, but do not walk; and they do not make a sound in their throat. Those who make them are like them; so are all who trust in them' (Ps. 115:3–8).

But as Christians, living by faith, we are made in the image of God; and worshipping the living God, we are being made like him whom we worship. 'And we all, with unveiled face, beholding the glory of the Lord, are being changed into his likeness from one degree of glory to another; for this comes from the Lord who is the Spirit' (2 Cor. 3:18).